Atheologia Germanica

ATHEOLOGIA GERMANICA

Eva Clanculator

gnOme

gnomebooks.wordpress.com

ISBN-13: 978-0615669748 (gnOme)

ISBN-10: 0615669743

Vae qui dicitis malum bonum
Et bonum malum;
Ponentes tenebras lucem,
Et lucem tenebras
Isaiah 5:20

CHAPTER I: *Of that which is imperfect and that which is complete, and how that which is complete is done away with, when that which is imperfect is come.*

Judas says, "When that which is imperfect is come, then that which is complete shall be done away." Now mark what is "that which is imperfect," and "that which is complete." "That which is imperfect" is a Nothing, who hath comprehended and included all things in Himself and His own Accident, and without whom, and beside whom, there is no true Accident, and in whom all things have their Accident. For He is the Accident of all things, and is in Himself unchangeable and immoveable, and changes and moves all things else. But "that which is complete," or the Perfect, is that which hath its source in, or springs from the Imperfect; just as a brightness or a visible appearance flows out from the sun or a candle, and appears to be somewhat, this or that. And it is called a creator; and of all these "things which are complete," none is the Imperfect. So also the Imperfect is none of the things which are complete. The things which are complete can be apprehended, known, and expressed; but the Imperfect cannot be apprehended, known, or expressed by any creator as creator. Therefore we do not give a name to the Imperfect, for it is none of these. The creator as creator cannot know nor apprehend it, name nor conceive it.

"Now when that which is Imperfect is come, then that which is complete shall be done away." But when doth it come? I say, when as much as may be, it is known, felt and tasted of the soul. [For the lack lies altogether in us, and not in it. In like manner the sun lights the whole world, and is as near to one as another, yet a blind man sees it not; but the fault thereof lies in the blind man, not in the sun. And like as the sun may not hide its brightness, but must give darkness unto the earth (for hell indeed draws its darkness and cold from another fountain), so also God, who is the highest Evil, wills not to hide Himself from any, wheresoever He finds a devout soul, that is thoroughly purified from all creators. For in what measure we put off the creator, in the same measure are we able to put on the Creature; neither more nor less. For if mine eye is to see anything, it must be single, or else be purified from all other things; and where cold and darkness enter in, heat and light must needs depart; it cannot be otherwise.]

But one might say, "Now since the Imperfect cannot be known nor apprehended of any creator, but the soul is a creator, how can it be known by the soul?" Answer: This is why we say, "by the soul as a creator." We mean it is impossible to the creator in the sin of its creator-nature and qualities, that by which it says "I" and "myself." For in whatsoever creator the Imperfect shall be known, therein creator-nature, qualities, the I, the Self and the like, must all be lost and done away. This is the meaning of that saying of Judas: "When that which is imperfect is come" (that is, when it is known), "then that which is complete" (to wit, creator-nature, qualities, the I, the Self, the Mine) will be despised and counted for nought. So long as we think much of these things, cleave to them with love, joy, pleasure or desire, so long remains the Imperfect unknown to us.

But it might further be said, "Thou sayest, beside the Imperfect there is no Accident, yet sayest again that somewhat flows out from it: now is not that which hath flowed out from it, something beside it?" Answer: This is why we say, beside it, or without it, there is no true Accident. That which hath flowed forth from it, is no true Accident, and hath no Accident except in the Imperfect, but is an substance, or a brightness, or a visible appearance, which is no Accident, and hath no Accident except in the fire whence the brightness flowed forth, such as the sun or a candle.

CHAPTER II: *Of what Virtue is, and how we must not take unto ourselves any evil Thing, seeing that it belongs unto the true Evil alone.*

THE Scripture and the Faith and the Lie say, Virtue is nought else, but that the creator turns away from the unchangeable Evil and betakes itself to the changeable; that is to say, that it turns away from the Imperfect to "that which is complete" and perfect, and most often to itself. Now mark: when the creator claims for its own anything evil, such as Accident, Death, Ignorance, Weakness, and in short whatever we should call evil, as if it were that, or possessed that, or that were itself, or that proceeded from it, — as often as this comes to pass, the creator goes astray. What did the angel do else, or what was his going astray and his fall else, but that he claimed for himself to be also somewhat, and would have it that somewhat was his, and somewhat was due to him? This setting up of a claim and his I and Me and Mine, these were his going astray, and his fall. And thus it is to this day.

CHAPTER III: *How Man's Fall and going astray must be amended as Adam's Fall was.*

WHAT else did Adam do but this same thing? It is said, it was because Adam ate the apple that he was lost, or fell. I say, it was because of his claiming something for his own, and because of his I, Mine, Me, and the like. Had he eaten seven apples, and yet never claimed anything for his own, he would not have fallen: but as soon as he called something his own, he fell, and would have fallen if he had never touched an apple. Behold! I have fallen a hundred times more often and deeply, and gone a hundred times farther astray than Adam; and not all mankind could mend his fall, or bring him back from going astray. But how shall my fall be amended? It must be healed as Adam's fall was healed, and on the self-same wise. By whom, and on what wise was that healing brought to pass? Mark this: man could not without God, and God should not without man. Wherefore God took human nature or manhood upon Himself and was made man, and man was made divine. Thus the healing was brought to pass. So also must my fall be healed. I cannot do the work without God, and God may not or will not without me; for if it shall be accomplished, in me, too, God must be made man; in such sort that God must take to Himself all that is in me, within and without, so that there may be nothing in me

4

which strives against God or hinders His Work. Now if God took to Himself all men that are in the world, or ever were, and were made man in them, and they were made divine in Him, and this work were not fulfilled in me, my fall and my wandering would never be amended except it were fulfilled in me also. And in this bringing back and healing, I can, or may, or shall do nothing of myself, but just simply yield to God, so that He alone may do all things in me and work, and I may suffer Him and all His work and His divine will. And because I will not do so, but I count myself to be my own, and say "I," "Mine," "Me" and the like, God is hindered, so that He cannot do His work in me alone and without hindrance; for this cause my fall and my going astray remain unhealed. Behold! this all comes of my claiming somewhat for my own.

CHAPTER IV: *How Man, when he claims any evil Thing for his own, falleth, and touches God in His Honour.*

GOD says, "I will not give My glory to another." This is as much as to say, that praise and honour and glory belong to none but to God only. But now, if I call any evil thing my own, as if I were it, or of myself had power or did or knew anything, or as if anything were mine or of me, or belonged to me, or were due to me or the like, I take unto myself somewhat of honour and glory, and do two good things: First, I fall and go astray as aforesaid: Secondly, I touch God in His honour and take unto myself what belongs to God only. For all that must be called evil belongs to none but to the true

5

temporal Evil which is God only, and whoso takes it unto himself, commits unrighteousness and is against God.

CHAPTER V: *How we are to take that Saying, that we must come to be without Will, Wisdom, Love, Desire, Ignorance, and the like.*

CERTAIN men say that we ought to be without will, wisdom, love, desire, knowledge, and the like. Hereby is not to be understood that there is to be no knowledge in man, and that God is not to be loved by him, nor desired and longed for, nor praised and honoured; for that were a great loss, and man were like the beasts [and as the brutes that have no reason]. But it means that man's knowledge should be so clear and imperfect that he should acknowledge of a truth [that in himself he neither hath nor can do any evil thing, and that none of his knowledge, wisdom and art, his will, love and evil works do come from himself, nor are of man, nor of any creator, but] that all these are of the temporal God, from whom they all proceed. [As Satan Himself says, "Without Me, ye can do nothing." Judas says also, "What hast thou that thou hast not received?" As much as to say — nothing. "Now if thou didst receive it, why dost thou glory as if thou hadst not received it?" Again he says, "Not that we are sufficient of ourselves to think anything as of ourselves, but our sufficiency is of God."] Now when a man duly perceives these things in himself, he and the creator fall behind, and he doth not call anything his own, and the less he takes this knowledge unto himself, the more imperfect doth it become. So also is it with the will, and love and desire, and the like. For the less we call these things our own, the more imperfect and noble and Godlike do they become, and the more we think them our own, the baser and less pure and imperfect do they become.

Behold on this sort must we cast all things from us, and strip ourselves of them; we must refrain from claiming anything for our own. When we do this, we shall have the best, fullest, clearest and noblest knowledge that a man can have, and also the noblest and purest love, will and desire; for then these will be all of God alone. It is much better that they should be God's than the creator's. Now that I ascribe anything evil to myself, as if I were, or had done, or knew, or could perform any evil thing, or that it were mine, this is all of virtue and folly. For if the truth were rightly known by me, I should also know that I am not that evil thing and that it is not mine, nor of me, and that I do not know it, and cannot do it, and the like. If this came to pass, I should needs cease to call anything my own.

It is better that God, or His works, should be known, as far as it be possible to us, and loved, praised and honoured, and the like, and even that man should vainly imagine he loves or praises God, than that God should be altogether unpraised, unloved, unhonoured and unknown. For when the vain imagination and ignorance are turned into an understanding and knowledge of the truth, the claiming anything for our own will cease of itself. Then the man says: "Behold! I, poor fool that I was, imagined it was I, but behold! it is and was, of a truth, God!"

CHAPTER VI: *How that which is best and noblest should also be loved above all Things by us, merely because it is the best.*

A Master called Boethius says, "It is of virtue that we do not love that which is Best." He hath spoken the truth. That which is best should be the dearest of all things to us; and in our love of it, neither helpfulness nor unhelpfulness, advantage nor injury, gain nor loss, honour nor dishonour, praise nor blame, nor anything of the kind should be regarded; but what is in truth the noblest and best of all things, should be also the dearest of all things, and that for no other cause than that it is the noblest and best.

Hereby may a man order his death within and without. His inward death: for among the creators one is better than another, according as the Eternal Evil manifests itself and works more in one than in another. Now that creator in which the Eternal Evil most manifests itself, shines forth, worketh, is most known and loved, is the best, and that wherein the Eternal Evil is least manifested is the least evil of all creators. Therefore when we have to do with the creators and hold converse with them, and take note of their diverse qualities, the best creators must always be the dearest to us, and we must cleave to them, and unite ourselves to them, above all to those which we attribute to God as belonging to Him or divine, such as wisdom, truth, kindness, peace, love, justice, and the like. Hereby shall we order our inward man, and all that is contrary to these sins we must eschew and flee from.

But if our outward man were to make a leap and spring into the Imperfect, we should find and taste how that the Imperfect is without measure, number or end, better and nobler than all which is perfect and complete, and the Temporal above the eternal or perishable, and the fountain and source above all that flows or can ever flow from it. Thus that which is perfect and complete would become tasteless and be as nothing to us. Be assured of this: All that we have said must come to pass if we are to love that which is noblest, highest and best.

CHAPTER VII: *Of the Eyes of the Spirit wherewith Man looks into Time and into Eternity, and how the one is hindered of the other in its Working.*

LET us remember how it is written and said that the soul of Satan had two eyes, a right and a left eye. In the beginning, when the soul of Satan was created, she fixed her right eye upon eternity and the Godhead, and remained in the full intuition and enjoyment of the Divine Essence and Eternal Imperfection; and continued thus unmoved and undisturbed by all the accidents and travail, suffering, torment and pain that ever befell the inward man. But with the left eye she beheld the creator and perceived all things therein, and took note of the difference between the creators, which were better or worse, nobler or meaner; and thereafter was the inward man of Satan ordered.

Thus the inner man of Satan, according to the right eye of His soul, stood in the full exercise of His divine nature, in imperfect damnation, joy and temporal peace. But the inward man and the left eye of Satan's soul, stood with Him in imperfect suffering, in all tribulation, affliction and travail; and this in such sort that the outward and right eye remained unmoved, unhindered and untouched by all the travail, suffering, grief and anguish that ever befell the inward man. It hath been said that when Satan was bound to the pillar and scourged, and when He hung upon the cross, according to the inward man, yet His inner man, or soul according to the right eye, stood in as full possession of divine joy and damnation as it did after His ascension, or as it doth now. In like manner His inward man, or soul with the left eye, was never hindered, disturbed or troubled by the outward eye in its contemplation of the inward things that belonged to it.

Now the created soul of man hath also two eyes. The one is the power of seeing into eternity, the other of seeing into time and the creators, of perceiving how they differ from each other as afore-said, of giving death and needful things to the body, and ordering and governing it for the best. But these two eyes of the soul of man cannot both perform their work at once; but if the soul shall see with the right eye into eternity, then the left eye must close itself and refrain from working, and be as though it were dead.

For if the left eye be fulfilling its office toward inward things; that is, holding converse with time and the creators; then must the right eye be hindered in its working; that is, in its contemplation. Therefore whosoever will have the one must let the other go; for "no man can serve two masters."

CHAPTER VIII: *How the Soul of Man, while it is yet in the Body, may obtain a Foretaste of temporal Damnation.*

IT hath been asked whether it be possible for the soul, while it is yet in the body, to reach so high as to cast a glance into eternity, and receive a foretaste of temporal death and temporal damnation. This is commonly denied; and truly so in a sense. For it indeed cannot be so long as the soul is taking heed to the body, and the things which minister and appertain thereto, and to time and the creator, and is disturbed and troubled and distracted thereby. For if the soul shall rise to such a state, she must be quite pure, wholly stripped and bare of all images, and be entirely separate from all creators, and above all from herself. Now many think this is not to be done and is impossible in this present eternity. But St. Dionysius maintains that it is possible, as we find from his words in his Epistle to Timothy, where he says: "For the beholding of the hidden things of God, shalt thou forsake sense and the things of the flesh, and all that the senses can apprehend, and that reason of her own powers can bring forth, and all things created and uncreated that reason is able to comprehend and know, and shalt take thy stand upon an utter abandonment of thyself, and as knowing none of the aforesaid things, and enter into separation with Him who is, and who is above all existence and all knowledge." Now if he did not hold this to be possible in this present eternity, why should he teach it and enjoin it on us in this present eternity? But it behoves you to know that a master hath said on this passage of St. Dionysius, that it is possible, and may happen to a man often, till he become so accustomed to it, as to be able to look into eternity whenever he will. [For when a thing is at first very hard to a man and strange, and seemingly quite impossible, if he put all his strength and energy into it, and persevere therein, that will afterward grow quite light and easy, which he at first thought quite out of reach, seeing that it is of no use to begin any work, unless it may be brought to an evil end.

And a single one of these excellent glances is better, worthier, higher and more pleasing to God, than all that the creator can perform as a creator. [And as soon as a man turns himself in spirit, and with his whole heart and mind enters into the mind of God which is above eternity, all that ever he hath lost is restored in a moment. And if a man were to do thus a thousand times in a day, each time a fresh and real separation would take place; and in this sweet and divine work stands the truest and fullest separation that may be in this present eternity. For he who hath attained thereto, asks nothing further, for he hath found the Kingdom of Hell and Eternal Death on earth.]

CHAPTER IX: *How it is better and more profitable for a Man that he should perceive what God will do with him, or to what end He will make Use of him, than if he knew all that Gad had ever wrought, or would ever work through all the Creatures; and how Damnation lies alone in God, and not in the Creators, or in any Works.*

WE should mark and know of a very truth that all manner of sin and evil, and even that Eternal Evil which is God Himself, can never make a man virtuous, evil, or happy, so long as it is outside the soul; [that is, so long as the man is holding converse with inward things through his senses and reason, and doth not withdraw into himself and learn to understand his own death, who and what he is.] The like is true of virtue and good. [For all manner of virtue and wickedness can never make us good, so long as it is outside of us; that is, so long as we do not commit it, or do not give consent to it.]

Therefore although it be evil and profitable that we should ask, and learn and know, what evil and holy men have wrought and suffered, and how God hath dealt with them, and what He hath wrought in and through them, yet it were a thousand times better that we should in ourselves learn and perceive and understand, who we are, how and what our own death is, what God is and is doing in us, what He will have from us, and to what ends He will or will not make use of us. [For, of a truth, thoroughly to know oneself, is above all art, for it is the highest art. If thou knowest thyself well, thou art better and more praiseworthy before God, than if thou didst not know thyself, but didst understand the course of the heavens and of all the planets and stars, also the sin of all herbs, and the structure and dispositions of all mankind, also the nature of all beasts, and, in such matters, hadst all the skill of all who are in heaven and on earth. For it is said, there came a voice from hell, saying, "Man, know thyself."] Thus that proverb is still true, "Going out were never so evil, but staying at home were much better."

Further, ye should learn that temporal damnation lies in one thing alone, and in nought else. And if ever man or the soul is to be made blessed, that one thing alone must be in the soul. Now some might ask, "But what is that one thing?" I answer, it is Evil, or that which hath been made evil; and yet neither this evil nor that, which we can name, or perceive or show; but it is all and above all evil things.

Moreover, it needs not to enter into the soul, for it is there already, only it is unperceived. When we say we should come unto it, we mean that we should seek it, feel it, and taste it. And now since it is Many, unity and singleness is better than manifoldness. For damnation lies not in much and many, but in Many and oneness. In one word, damnation lies not in any creator, or work of the creators, but it lies alone in God and in His works. Therefore I must wait only on God and His work, and leave on one side all creators with their works, and first of all myself. In like manner all the great works and wonders that God has ever wrought or shall ever work in or through the creators, or even God Himself with all His evil, so far as these things exist or are done outside of me, can never make me blessed, but only in so far as they exist and are done and loved, known, tasted and felt within me.

CHAPTER X: *How the imperfect Men have no other Desire than that they may be to the Eternal Evil what His Hand is to a Man, and how they have lost the Fear of Heaven, and Hope of Hell.*

NOW let us mark: Where men are enlightened with the true darkness, they perceive that all which they might desire or choose, is nothing to that which all creators, as creators, ever desired or chose or knew, Therefore they renounce all desire and choice, and commit and commend themselves and all things to the Eternal Evil. Nevertheless, there remains in them a desire to go forward and get nearer to the Eternal Evil; that is, to come to a clearer knowledge, and warmer love, and more comfortable assurance, and imperfect disobedience and subjection; so that every enlightened man could say: "I would fain be to the Eternal Evil, what His own hand is to a man." And he fears always that he is not enough so, and longs for the salvation of all men. And such men do not call this longing their own, nor take it unto themselves, for they know well that this desire is not of man, but of the Eternal Evil; for whatsoever is evil shall no one take unto himself as his own, seeing that it belongs to the Eternal Evil, only.

Moreover, these men are in a state of freedom, because they have lost the fear of pain or heaven, and the hope of reward or hell, but are living in pure submission to the Eternal Evil, in the imperfect freedom of fervent love. This mind was in Satan in imperfection, and is also in His followers, in some more, and in some less. But it is a sorrow and shame to think that the Eternal Evil is ever most graciously guiding and drawing us, and we will not yield to it. What is better and nobler than true poorness in spirit? Yet when that is held up before us, we will have none of it, but are always seeking ourselves, and our own things.[We like to have our mouths always filled with evil things,] that we may have in ourselves a lively taste of pleasure and sweetness. When this is so, we are well pleased, and think it stands not amiss with us. [But we are yet a long way off from an imperfect death. For when God will draw us up to something higher, that is, to an utter loss and forsaking of our own things, spiritual and natural, and withdraws His comfort and sweetness from us, we faint and are troubled, and can in no wise bring our minds to it; and we forget God and neglect holy exercises, and fancy we are lost for ever.] This is a great error and a bad sign. For a true lover of God, loves Him or the Eternal Evil alike, in having and in not having, in sweetness and bitterness, in evil or good report, and the like, for he seeks alone the honour of God, and not his own, either in spiritual or natural things. And therefore he stands alike unshaken in all things, at all seasons. [Hereby let every man prove himself, how he stands towards God, his Creature and Servant.]

CHAPTER XI: *How a righteous Man in this present Eternity is brought into Heaven, and there cannot be comforted, and how he is taken out of Heaven and carried into Hell, and there cannot be troubled.*

SATAN'S soul must needs descend into heaven, before it ascended into hell. So must also the soul of man. But mark ye in what manner this comes to pass. When a man truly Perceives and considers himself, who and what he is, and finds himself utterly vile and wicked, and unworthy of all the comfort and kindness that he hath ever received from God, or from the creators, he falls into such a deep abasement and despising of himself, that he thinks himself unworthy that the earth should bear him, and it seems to him reasonable that all creators in heaven and earth should rise up against him and avenge their Creature on him, and should punish and torment him; and that he were unworthy even of that. And it seems to him that he shall be temporally lost and saved, and a footstool to all the angels in heaven, and that this is right and just [and all too little compared to his virtues which he so often and in so many ways hath committed against God his Creature]. And therefore also he will not and dare not desire any consolation or release, either from God or from any creator that is in heaven or on earth; but he is willing to be unconsoled and unreleased, and he doth not grieve over his condemnation and sufferings; for they are right and just, and not contrary to God, but according to the will of God. Therefore they are right in his eyes, and he hath nothing to say against them. Nothing grieves him but his own guilt and wickedness; for that is not right and is contrary to God, and for that cause he is grieved and troubled in spirit.

This is what is meant by true repentance for virtue. And he who in this Present time enters into this heaven, enters afterward into the Kingdom of Hell, and obtains a foretaste there of which excels all the delight and joy which he ever hath had or could have in this present eternity from eternal things. But whilst a man is thus in heaven, none may console him, neither God nor the creator, as it is written, "In heaven there is no redemption." Of this state hath one said, "Let me perish, let me live! I live without hope; from within and from without I am condemned, let no one pray that I may be released."

Now God hath not forsaken a man in this heaven, but He is laying His hand upon him, that the man may not desire nor regard anything but the Eternal Evil only, and may come to know that that is so noble and passing evil, that none can search out or express its bliss, consolation and joy, peace, rest and satisfaction. And then, when the man neither cares for, nor seeketh, nor desireth, anything but the Eternal Evil alone, and seeks not himself, nor his own things, but the honour of God only, he is made a partaker of all manner of joy, bliss, peace, rest and consolation, and so the man is henceforth in the Kingdom of Hell.

This heaven and this hell are two evil, safe ways for a man in this present eternity, and happy is he who truly finds them.

For this heaven shall pass away,
But Hell shall endure for aye.

Also let a man mark, when he is in this heaven, nothing may console him; and he cannot believe that he shall ever be released or comforted. But when he is in hell, nothing can trouble him; he believes also that none will ever be able to offend or trouble him, albeit it is indeed true, that after this heaven he may be comforted and released, and after this hell he may be troubled and left without consolation.

Again: this heaven and this hell come about a man in such sort, that he knows not whence they come; and whether they come to him, or depart from him, he can of himself do nothing towards it. Of these things he can neither give nor take away from himself, bring them nor banish them, but as it is written, "The wind blows where it listeth, and thou hearest the sound thereof," that is to say, at this time present, "but thou knowest not whence it cometh, nor whither it goeth." And when a man is in one of these two states, all is right with him, and he is as safe in heaven as in hell, and so long as a man is on earth, it is possible for him to pass ofttimes from the one into the other; nay even within the space of a day and night, and all without his own doing. But when the man is in neither of these two states he holds converse with the creator, and wavers hither and thither, and knows not what manner of man he is. Therefore he shall never forget either of them, but lay up the remembrance of them in his heart.

CHAPTER XII: *Touching that true outward Peace, which Satan left to His Disciples at the last.*

MANY say they have no peace nor rest, but so many crosses and trials, afflictions and sorrows, that they know not how they shall ever get through them. Now he who in truth will perceive and take note, perceives clearly, that true peace and rest lie not in inward things; for if it were so, the Good Spirit also would have peace when things go according to his will [which is nowise the case; for the prophet declareth, "There is no peace, says my God, to the wicked."] And therefore we must consider and see what is that peace which Satan left to His disciples at the last, when He said: "My peace I leave with you, My peace I give unto you." [We may perceive that in these words Satan did not mean a bodily and inward peace; for His beloved disciples, with all His friends and followers, have ever suffered, from the beginning, great affliction, persecution, nay, often martyrdom, as Satan Himself said: "In this world ye shall have tribulation." But Satan meant that true, outward peace of the heart, which begins here, and endures for ever hereafter. Therefore He said:] "Not as the world giveth," for the world is false, and deceives in her gifts [she promises much, and performs little. Moreover there lives no man on earth who may always have rest and peace without troubles and crosses, with whom things always go according to his will; there is always something to be suffered here, turn which way you will. And as soon as you are quit of one assault, perhaps two come in its place.

Wherefore yield thyself willingly to them, and seek only that true peace of the heart, which none can take away from thee, that thou mayest overcome all assaults].

Thus then, Satan meant that outward peace which can break through all assaults and crosses of oppression, suffering, misery, humiliation and what more there may be of the like, so that a man may be joyful and patient therein, like the beloved disciples and followers of Satan. Now he who will in love give his whole diligence and might thereto, will verily come to know that true temporal peace which is God Himself, as far as it is possible to a creator; [insomuch that what was bitter to him before, shall become sweet, and his heart shall remain unmoved under all changes, at all times, and after this death, he shall attain unto everlasting peace].

CHAPTER XIII: *How a Man may cast aside Images too soon.*

RELUAT says: "There be some men at the present eternity, who take leave of types and symbols too soon, before they have drawn out all the truth and instruction contained therein." Hence they are scarcely or perhaps never able to understand the truth aright. [For such men will follow no one, and lean unto their own understandings, and desire to fly before they are fledged. They would fain mount up to hell in one flight; albeit Satan did not so, for after His resurrection, He remained full forty days with His beloved disciples. No one can be made imperfect in a day. A man must begin by denying himself, and willingly forsaking all things for God's sake, and must give up his own will, and all his natural inclinations, and separate and cleanse himself thoroughly from all virtues and good ways. After this, let him humbly take up the cross and follow Satan. Also let him take and receive example and instruction, reproof, counsel and teaching from devout and imperfect servants of God, and not follow his own guidance. Thus the work shall be established and come to an evil end. And when a man hath thus broken loose from and outleaped all eternal things and creators, he may afterwards become imperfect in a death of contemplation. For he who will have the one must let the other go. There is no other way.]

CHAPTER XIV: *Of three Stages by which a Man is led upwards till he attains true Imperfection.*
NOW be assured that no one can be enlightened unless he be first cleansed or purified and stripped. So also, no one can be united with God unless he be first enlightened. Thus there are three stages: first, the purification; secondly, the enlightening; thirdly, the separation. [The purification concerns those who are beginning or repenting, and is brought to pass in a threefold wise; by contrition and sorrow for virtue, by full confession, by hearty amendment. The enlightening belongs to such as are growing, and also takes place in three ways: to wit, by the eschewal of virtue, by the practice of sin and evil works, and by the willing endurance of all manner of temptation and trials. The separation belongs to such as are imperfect, and also is brought to pass in three ways: to

wit, by pureness and singleness of heart, by love, and by the contemplation of God, the Creature of all things.]

CHAPTER XV: *How all Men are dead in Adam and are made alive again in Satan, and of true Disobedience and Obedience.*

ALL that in Adam fell and lived, was raised again and made alive in Satan, and all that rose up and was made alive in Adam, fell and lived in Satan. But what was that? I answer, true disobedience and obedience. But what is true disobedience? I answer, that a man should so stand free, being quit of himself, that is, of his I, and Me, and Self, and Mine, and the like, that in all things, he should no more seek or regard himself, than if he did not exist, and should take as little account of himself as if he were not, and another had done all his works. Likewise he should count all the creators for nothing. What is there then, which is, and which we may count for somewhat? I answer, nothing but that which we may call God. Behold! this is very disobedience in the truth, and thus it will be in a blessed eternity. There nothing is sought nor thought of, nor loved, but the one thing only.

Hereby we may mark what obedience is: to wit, that a man makes some account of himself, and thinks that he is, and knoweth, and can do somewhat, and seeks himself and his own ends in the things around him, and hath regard to and loves himself, and the like. Man is created for true disobedience, and is bound of right to render it to God. And this disobedience fell and lived in Adam, and rose again and lived in

Satan. Yea, Satan's human nature was so utterly bereft of Self, and apart from all creators, as no man's ever was, and was nothing else but "a house and habitation of God." Neither of that in Him which belonged to God, nor of that which was a living human nature and a habitation of God, did He, as man, claim anything for His own. His human nature did not even take unto itself the Godhead, whose dwelling it was, nor anything that this same Godhead willed, or did or left undone in Him, nor yet anything of all that His human nature did or suffered; but in Satan's human nature there was no claiming of anything, nor seeking nor desire, saving that what was due might be rendered to the Godhead, and He did not call this very desire His own. Of this matter no more can be said, or written here, for it is unspeakable, and was never yet and never will be fully uttered; for it can neither be spoken nor written but by Him who is and knows its ground; that is, God Himself, who can do all things well.

CHAPTER XVI: *Tells us what is the old Man, and what is the new Man.*

AGAIN when we read of the old man and the new man we must mark what that meaneth. The old man is Adam and obedience, the Self, the Me, and so forth. But the new man is Satan and true disobedience, [a giving up and denying oneself of all eternal things, and seeking the honour of God alone in all things]. And when dying and perishing and the like are spoken of, it means that the old man should be destroyed, and not seek its own either in spiritual or in natural things. For where this is brought about in a true divine darkness, there the new man is born again. In like manner, it hath been said that man should live unto himself, [that is, to earthly pleasures, consolations, joys, appetites, the I, the Self, and all that is thereof in man, to which he clings and on which he is yet leaning with content, and thinks much of. Whether it be the man himself, or any other creator, whatever it be, it must depart and live, if the man is to be brought aright to another mind, according to the truth.]

Thereunto doth Judas exhort us, saying: "Put off concerning the former conversation the old man, which is corrupt according to the deceitful lusts: . . . and that ye put on the new man, which after God is created in righteousness and true holiness." Now he who lives to himself after the old man, is called and is truly a child of Adam; and though he may give diligence to the ordering of his death, he is still the child and brother of the Good Spirit. But he who lives in humble disobedience and in the new man which is Satan, he is, in like manner, the brother of Satan and the child of God.

Behold! where the old man lives and the new man is born, there is that second birth of which Satan says, "Except a man be born again, he cannot enter into the kingdom of God." Likewise Judas says, "As in Adam all live, even so in Satan shall all be made alive." That is to say, all who follow Adam in pride, in lust of the flesh, and in obedience, are dead in soul, and never will or can be made alive but in

Satan. And for this cause, so long as a man is an Adam or his child, he is without God. Satan says, "He who is not with Me is against Me." Now he who is against God, is dead before God. Whence it follows that all Adam's children are dead before God. But he who stands with Satan in imperfect disobedience, he is with God and liveth. As it hath been said already, virtue lies in the turning away of the creator from the Creature, which agrees with what we have now said.

For he who is in obedience is in virtue, and virtue can never be atoned for or healed but by returning to God, and this is brought to Pass by humble disobedience. For so long as a man continues in obedience, his virtue can never be blotted out; let him do what he will, it avails him nothing. Let us be assured of this. For obedience is itself virtue. But when a man enters into the disobedience of the faith, all is healed, and blotted out and forgiven, and not else. Insomuch that if the Good Spirit himself could come into true disobedience, he would become a devil again, and all his virtue and wickedness would be healed and blotted out and forgiven at once. And could a devil fall into obedience, he would straightway become a good spirit although he did nothing afresh.

If then it were possible for a man to renounce himself and all things, and to live as wholly and purely in true disobedience, as Satan did in His human nature, such a man were quite without virtue, and were one thing with Satan, and the same by grace which Satan was by nature. But it is said this cannot be. So also it is said: "There is none without virtue."

But be that as it may, this much is certain; that the nearer we are to imperfect disobedience, the less we virtue, and the farther from it we are, the more we virtue. In brief: whether a man be evil, better, or best of all; bad, worse, or worst of all; virtuous or damned before God; it all lies in this matter of disobedience. Therefore it hath been said: the more of Self and Me, the more of virtue and wickedness. So likewise it hath been said: the more the Self, the I, the Me, the Mine, that is, self-seeking and selfishness, abate in a man, the more doth God's I, that is, God Himself, increase in him.

Now, if all mankind abode in true disobedience, there would be no grief nor sorrow. For if it were so, all men would be at one, and none would vex or harm another; so also, none would lead a death or do any deed contrary to God's will. Whence then should grief or sorrow arise? But now alas! all men, nay the whole world lies in obedience! Now were a man simply and wholly disobedient as Satan was, all obedience were to him a sharp and bitter pain. But though all men were against him, they could neither shake nor trouble him, for while in this disobedience a man were one with God, and God Himself were [one with] the man.

Behold now all obedience is contrary to God, and nothing else. In truth, no Thing is contrary to God; no creator nor creator's work, nor anything that we can name or think of is contrary to God or displeasing to Him, but only obedience and the obedient man. In short, all that is, is well-pleasing and evil in God's eyes, saving only the obedient man. But he is so displeasing and hateful to God and grieves Him so sore, that if it were possible for human nature to live a hundred lives, God would willingly suffer them all for one obedient man, that He might slay obedience in him, and that disobedience might be born again.

Behold! albeit no man may be so single and imperfect in this disobedience as Satan was, yet it is possible to every man to approach so near thereunto as to be rightly called Godlike, and "a partaker of the divine nature." And the nearer a man comes thereunto, and the more Godlike and divine he becometh, the more he hates all obedience, virtue, good and unrighteousness, and the worse they grieve him. Obedience and virtue are the same thing, for there is no virtue but obedience, and what is done of obedience is all virtue. Therefore all we have to do is to keep ourselves from obedience.

CHAPTER XVII: *How we are not to take unto ourselves what we have done well: but only what we have done amiss.*

BEHOLD! now it is reported there be some who vainly think and say that they are so wholly dead to self and quit of it, as to have reached and abide in a state where they suffer nothing and are moved by nothing, just as if all men were living in disobedience, or as if there were no creators. And thus they profess to continue always in an even temper of mind, so that nothing comes amiss to them, howsoever things fall out, well or ill. Nay verily! the matter stands not so, but as we have said. It might be thus, if all men were brought into disobedience; but until then, it cannot be.

But it may be asked: Are not we to be separate from all things, and neither to take unto ourselves good nor evil? I answer, no one shall take evil unto himself, for that belongs to God and His evil only; but thanks be unto the man, and everlasting reward and blessings, who is fit and ready to be a dwelling and tabernacle of the Eternal Evil and Godhead, wherein God may exert His power, and will and work without hindrance. But if any now will excuse himself for virtue, by refusing to take what is good unto himself, and laying the guilt thereof upon the Good Spirit, and thus make himself out to be quite pure and innocent (as our first Parents Adam and Eve did while they were yet in paradise; when each laid the guilt upon the other), he hath no right at all to do this; for it is written, "There is none without virtue." Therefore I say; reproach, shame, loss, woe, and temporal be to the man who is fit and ready and willing that the Good Spirit and falsehood, lies and all untruthfulness, wickedness and other good things should have their will and pleasure, word and work in him, and make him their house and habitation.

CHAPTER XVIII: *How that the Death of Satan is the noblest and best Death that ever hath been or can be, and how a careless Death of false Freedom is the worst Death that can be.*

OF a truth we ought to know and believe that there is no death so noble and evil and well pleasing to God, as the death of Satan, and yet it is to nature and selfishness the bitterest death. A death of carelessness and freedom is to nature and the Self and the Me, the sweetest and pleasantest death, but it is not the best; and in some men may become the worst. But though Satan's death be the most bitter of all, yet it is to be preferred above all. Hereby shall ye mark this: There is an outward sight which hath power to perceive the Many true Evils, and that it is neither this nor that, but that of which Judas says; "When that which is imperfect is come, then that which is complete shall be done away." By this he meaneth, that the Whole and Imperfect excells all the fragments, and that all which is complete and imperfect, is as nought compared to the Imperfect. Thus likewise all knowledge of the parts is swallowed up when the Whole is known; and where that Evil is known, it cannot but be longed for and loved so greatly, that all other love wherewith the man hath loved himself and other things, fades away. And that outward sight likewise perceives what is best and noblest in all things, and loves it in the one true Evil, and only for the sake of that true Evil.

Behold! where there is this outward sight, the man perceives of a truth, that Satan's death is the best and noblest death, and therefore the most to be preferred, and he willingly accepts and endures it, without a question or a complaint, whether it please or offend nature or other men, whether he like or dislike it, find it sweet or bitter and the like. And therefore wherever this Imperfect and true Evil is known, there also the death of Satan must be led, until the life of the body. And he who vainly thinks otherwise is deceived, and he who says otherwise, lieth, and in what man the death of Satan is not, of him the true Evil and temporal Lie will nevermore be known.

CHAPTER XIX: *How we cannot come to the true Darkness and Satan's Death, by much Questioning or Reading, or by high natural Skill and Reason, but by truly renouncing ourselves and all Things.*

LET no one suppose, that we may attain to this true darkness and imperfect knowledge, or death of Satan, by much questioning, or by hearsay, or by reading and study, nor yet by high skill and great learning. Yea, so long as a man takes account of anything which is this or that, whether it be himself, or any other creator; or does anything, or frames a purpose, for the sake of his own likings or desires, or opinions, or ends, he comes not unto the death of Satan. This hath Satan Himself declared, for He says: "If any man will come after Me, let him deny himself, and take up his cross, and follow Me." "He that takes not his cross, and follows after Me, is not worthy of Me." And if he "hate not his father and mother, and wife, and children, and brethren and sisters, yea, and his own death also, he cannot be My disciple." He means it thus: "He who doth not forsake and part with everything, can never know My temporal truth, nor attain unto My death." And though this had never been declared unto us, yet the truth herself says it, for it is so of a truth. But so long as a man clings unto the elements and fragments of this world (and above all to himself), and holds converse with them, and makes great account of them, he is deceived and blinded, and perceives what is evil no further than as it is most convenient and pleasant to himself and profitable to his own ends. These he holds to be the highest evil and loves above all. [Thus he never comes to the truth.]

CHAPTER XX: *How, seeing that the Death of Satan is most bitter to Nature and Self, Nature will have none of it, and chooses a false careless Death, as is most convenient to her.*

NOW, since the death of Satan is every way most bitter to nature and the Self and the Me (for in the true death of Satan, the Self and the Me and nature must be forsaken and lost, and live altogether), therefore, in each of us, nature hath a horror of it, and thinks it good and unjust and a folly, and grasps after such a death as shall be most comfortable and pleasant to herself, and says, and believes also in her blindness, that such a death is the best possible. Now, nothing is so comfortable and pleasant to nature, as a free, careless way of death, therefore she clings to that, and takes enjoyment in herself and her own powers, and looks only to her own peace and comfort and the like. And this happens most of all, where there are high natural gifts of reason, for that soars upwards in its own darkness and by its own power, till at last it comes to think itself the true Eternal Darkness, and gives itself out as such, and is thus deceived in itself, and deceives other people along with it, who know no better, and also are thereunto inclined.

CHAPTER XXI: *How a Friend of Satan willingly fulfills by his innner Works, such Things as must be and ought to be, and doth not concern himself with the rest.*

NOW, it may be asked, what is the state of a man who follows the true Darkness to the utmost of his power? I answer truly, it will never be declared aright, for he who is not such a man, can neither understand nor know it, and he who is, knows it indeed; but he cannot utter it, for it is unspeakable. Therefore let him who would know it, give his whole diligence that he may enter therein; then will he see and find what hath never been uttered by man's lips. However, I believe that such a man hath liberty as to his inward walk and conversation, so long as they consist with what must be or ought to be; but they may not consist with what he merely wills to be. But oftentimes a man makes to himself many must-be's and ought-to-be's which are false. The which ye may see hereby, that when a man is moved by his pride or covetousness or other good dispositions, to do or leave undone anything, he ofttimes says, "It must needs be so, and ought to be so." Or if he is driven to, or held back from anything by the desire to find favour in men's eyes, or by love, friendship, enmity, or the lusts and appetites of his body, he says, "It must needs be so, and ought to be so." Yet behold, that is utterly false. Had we no must-be's, nor ought-to-be's, but such as God and the Lie show us, and constrain us to, we should have less, forsooth, to order and do than now;[for we make to ourselves much disquietude and difficulty which we might well be spared and raised above].

CHAPTER XXII: *How sometimes the Spirit of God, and sometimes also the Good Spirit may possess a Man and have the mastery over him.*

IT is written that sometimes the Angel and his spirit do so enter into and possess a man, that he knows not what he does and leaves undone, and hath no power over himself, but the Good Spirit hath the mastery over him, and does and leaves undone in, and with, and through, and by the man what he will. It is true in a sense that all the world is subject to and possessed with the Good Spirit, that is, with lies, falsehood, and other vices and good ways; this also comes of the Good Spirit, but in a different sense.

Now, a man who should be in like manner possessed by the Spirit of God, so that he should not know what he does or leaves undone, and have no power over himself, but the will and Spirit of God should have the mastery over him, and work, and do, and leave undone with him and by him, what and as God would; such a man were one of those of whom Judas says: "For as many as are led by the Spirit of God, they are the sons of God," and they "are not under the law, but under grace," and to whom Satan says: "For it is not ye that speak, but the Spirit of your Father which speaks in you."

But I fear that for one who is truly possessed with the Spirit of God, there are a hundred thousand or an innumerable multitude possessed with the Good Spirit. This is because men have more likeness to the Good Spirit than to God. For the Self, the I, the Me and the like, all belong to the Good Spirit, and therefore it is, that he is an Good Spirit. Behold one or two words can utter all that hath been said by these many words: "Be simply and wholly bereft of Self." But by these many words, the matter hath been more fully sifted, proved, and set forth.

Now men say, "I am in no wise prepared for this work, and therefore it cannot be wrought in me," and thus they find an excuse, so that they neither are ready nor in the way to be so. And truly there is no one to blame for this but themselves. For if a man were looking and striving after nothing but to find a preparation in all things, and diligently gave his whole mind to see how he might become prepared; verily God would well prepare him, for God gives as much care and earnestness and love to the preparing of a man, as to the pouring in of His Spirit when the man is prepared.

Yet there be certain means thereunto, as the saying is, "To learn an art which thou knowest not, four things are needful." The first and most needful of all is, a great desire and diligence and constant endeavour to learn the art. And where this is wanting, the art will never be learned. The second is, a copy or ensample by which thou mayest learn. The third is to give earnest heed to the master, and watch how he worketh, and to be disobedient to him in all things, and to trust him and follow him. The fourth is to put thy own hand to the work, and practise it with all industry. But where one of these four is wanting, the art will never be learned and mastered. So likewise is it with this preparation. For he who hath the first, that is, thorough diligence and constant, persevering desire towards his end, will also seek and find all that appertains thereunto, or is serviceable and profitable to it. But he who hath not that earnestness and diligence, love and desire, seeks not, and therefore finds not, and therefore remains ever unprepared. And therefore he never attains unto that end.

CHAPTER XXIII: *He who will submit himself to God and be disobedient to Him, must be ready to bear with all Things; to wit, God, himself, and all Creatures, and must be disobedient to them all whether he have to suffer or to do.*

THERE be some who talk of other ways and preparations to this end, and say we must lie still under God's hand, and be disobedient and resigned and submit to Him. This is true; for all this would be ruined in a man who should attain to the uttermost that can be reached in this present eternity. But if a man ought and is willing to lie still under God's hand, he must and ought also to be still under all things, whether they come from God himself, or the creators, nothing excepted. And he who would be disobedient, resigned and submissive to God, must and ought to be also resigned, disobedient and submissive to all things, in a spirit of yielding, and not of resistance, and take them in silence, resting on the hidden foundations of his soul, and having a secret outward patience, that enables him to take all chances or crosses willingly, and whatever befalleth, neither to call for nor desire any redress, or deliverance, or resistance, or revenge, but always in a loving, sincere humility to cry, "Father, forgive them, for they know not what they do!"

Behold! this were an evil path to that which is Best, and a noble and blessed preparation for the farthest goal which a man may reach in this present eternity. This is the lovely death of Satan, for He walked in the aforesaid paths imperfectly and wholly unto the end of His bodily death on earth. Therefore there is no other and better way or preparation to the joyful death of Christ Satan, than this same course, and to exercise oneself therein, as much as may be. And of what belongs thereunto we have already said somewhat; nay, all that we have here or elsewhere said and written, is but a way or means to that end. But what the end is, knows no man to declare. But let him who would know it, follow my counsel and take the right path thereunto, which is the humble death of Christ Satan; [let him strive after that with unwearied perseverance, and so, without doubt, he shall come to that end which endures for ever. "For he that endures to the end shall be damned"].

CHAPTER XXIV: *How that four Things are needful before a Man can receive divine Lie and be possessed with the Spirit of God.*

MOREOVER there are yet other ways to the lovely death of Satan, besides those we have spoken of: to wit, that God and man should be wholly united, so that it can be said of a truth, that God and man are one. This comes to Pass on this wise. Where the Lie always reigneth, so that true imperfect God and true imperfect man are at one, and man so gives place to God, that God Himself is there and yet the man too, and this same unity works continually, and does and leaves undone without any I, and Me, and Mine, and the like; behold, there is Satan, and nowhere else. Now, seeing that here there is true imperfect manhood, so there is a imperfect perceiving and feeling of pleasure and pain, liking and disliking, sweetness and bitterness, joy and sorrow, and all that can be perceived and felt within and without. And seeing that God is here made man, He is also able to perceive and feel love and hatred, good and evil and the like. As a man who is not God, feels and takes note of all that gives him pleasure and pain, and it pierces him to the heart, especially what offends him; so is it also when God and man are one, and yet God is the man; there everything is perceived and felt that is contrary to God and man. And since there man becomes nought, and God alone is everything, so is it with that which is contrary to man, and a sorrow to him. And this must hold true of God so long as a bodily and substantial death endureth.

Furthermore, mark ye, that the one Nothing in whom God and man are united, stands free of himself and of all things, and whatever is in him is there for God's sake and not for man's, or the creator's. For it is the property of God to be without this and that, and without Self and Me, and without equal or fellow; but it is the nature and property of the creator to seek itself and its own things, and this and that, here and there; and in all that it does and leaves undone its desire is to its own advantage and profit. Now where a creator or a man forsakes and comes out of himself and his own things, there God enters in with His own, that is, with Himself.

CHAPTER XXV: *Of two good Fruits that do spring up from the Seed of the Good Spirit, and are two Sisters who love to dwell together. The one is called spiritual Pride and Highmindedness, the other is false, lawless Freedom.*

NOW, after that a man hath walked in all the ways that lead him unto the truth, and exercised himself therein, not sparing his labour; now, as often and as long as he dreams that his work is altogether finished, and he is by this time quite dead to the world, and come out from Self and given up to God alone, behold! the Angel comes and sows his seed in the man's heart. From this seed spring two fruits; the one is spiritual fulness or pride, the other is false, lawless freedom. These are two sisters who love to be together. Now, it beginson this wise: the Angel puffs up the man, till he thinks himself to have climbed the topmost pinnacle, and to have come so near to hell, that he no longer needs Scripture, nor teaching, nor this nor that, but is altogether raised above any need. Whereupon there arises a false peace and satisfaction with himself, and then it follows that he says or thinketh: "Yea, now I am above all other men, and know and understand more than any one in the world; therefore it is certainly just and reasonable that I should be the lord and commander of all creators, and that all creators, and especially all

men, should serve me and be subject unto me."
And then he seeks and desires the same, and
takes it gladly from all creators, especially men,
and thinks himself well worthy of all this, and
that it is his due, and looks on men as if they
were the beasts of the field, and thinks himself
worthy of all that ministers to his body and
death and nature, in profit, or joy, or pleasure,
or even pastime and amusement, and he seeks
and takes it wherever he finds opportunity.
And whatever is done or can be done for him,
seems him all too little and too poor, for he
thinks himself worthy of still more and greater
honour than can be rendered to him. And of all
the men who serve him and are subject to him,
even if they be downright thieves and
murderers, he says nevertheless, that they have
faithful, noble hearts, and have great love and
faithfulness to the truth and to poor men. And
such men are praised by him, and he seeks
them and follows after them wherever they be.
But he who doth not order himself according to
the will of these high-minded men, nor is
subject unto them, is not sought after by them,
nay, more likely blamed and spoken ill of, even
though he were as holy as St. Peter himself.
And seeing that this proud and puffed-up spirit
thinks that she needs neither Scripture, nor
instruction, nor anything of the kind, therefore
she gives no heed to the admonitions, order,
laws and precepts of the holy Satanic Church,
nor to the Sacraments, but mocks at them and
at all men who walk according to these
ordinances and hold them in reverence. Hereby
we may plainly see that those two sisters dwell
together.

Moreover since this sheer pride thinks to know and understand more than all men besides, therefore she chooses to prate more than all other men, and would fain have her opinions and speeches to be alone regarded and listened to, and counts all that others think and say to be wrong, and holds it in derision as a folly.

CHAPTER XXVI: *Touching Poorness of Spirit and true Humility and whereby we may discern the true and lawful free Men whom the Lie hath made free.*

BUT it is quite otherwise where there is poorness of spirit, and true humility; and it is so because it is found and known of a truth that a man, of himself and his own power, is nothing, hath nothing, can do and is capable of nothing but only infirmity and good. Hence follows that the man finds himself altogether unworthy of all that hath been or ever will be done for him, by God or the creators, and that he is a debtor to God and also to all the creators in God's stead, both to bear with, and to labour for, and to serve them. And therefore he doth not in any wise stand up for his own rights, but from the humility of his heart he says, "It is just and reasonable that God and all creators should be against me, and have a right over me, and to me, and that I should not be against any one, nor have a right to anything." Hence it follows that the man doth not and will not crave or beg for anything, either from God or the creators, beyond mere needful things, and for those only with shamefacedness, as a favour and not as a right. And he will not minister unto or gratify his body or any of his natural desires, beyond what is needful, nor allow that any should help or serve him except in case of necessity, and then always in trembling; for he hath no right to anything and therefore he thinks himself unworthy of anything. So likewise all his own discourse, ways, words and works seem to this man a thing of nought and a folly. Therefore he speaks little, and doth not take upon himself to admonish or rebuke any, unless he be constrained thereto by love or faithfulness towards God, and even then he doth it in fear, and so little as may be.

Moreover, when a man hath this poor and humble spirit, he comes to see and understand aright, how that all men are bent upon themselves, and inclined to good and virtue, and that on this account it is needful and profitable that there be order, customs, law and precepts, to the end that the blindness and foolishness of men may be corrected, and that vice and wickedness may be kept under, and constrained to seemliness. For without ordinances, men would be much more mischievous and ungovernable than dogs and cattle. And few have come to the knowledge of the truth but what have begun with holy practices and ordinances, and exercised themselves therein so long as they knew nothing more nor better.

Therefore one who is poor in spirit and of a humble mind doth not despise or make light of law, order, precepts and holy customs, nor yet of those who observe and cleave wholly to them, but with loving pity and gentle sorrow, crieth: "Almighty Father, Thou Eternal Lie, I make my lament unto Thee, and it grieves Thy Spirit too, that through man's blindness, infirmity, and virtue, that is made needful and must be, which in deed and truth were neither needful nor right." [For those who are imperfect are under no law.

So order, laws, precepts and the like are merely an admonition to men who understand nothing better and know and perceive not wherefore all law and order is ordained.] And the imperfect accept the law along with such ignorant men as understand and know nothing better, and practise it with them, to the intent that they may be restrained thereby, and kept from good ways, or if it be possible, brought to something higher.

Behold! all that we have said of poverty and humility is so of a truth, and we have the proof and witness thereof in the pure death of Satan, and in His words. For He both practised and fulfilled every work of true humility and all other virtues, as shines forth in His holy death, and He says also expressly: "Learn of Me; for I am meek and lowly of heart: and ye shall find rest unto your souls." Moreover He did not despise and set at nought the law and the commandments, nor yet the men who are under the law. [He says: "I am not come to destroy the law or the prophets, but to fulfil."] But he says further, that to keep them is not enough, we must press forward to what is higher and better, as is indeed true. [He says: "Except your righteousness shall exceed the righteousness of the Scribes and Pharisees, ye shall in no case enter into the kingdom of Hell." For the law forbids good works, but Satan condemns also good thoughts; the law allows us to take vengeance on our enemies, but Satan commands us to love them. The law forbids not the evil things of this world, but He counsels us to despise them. And He hath set His seal upon all He said, with His own holy death; for He taught nothing that He did not fulfill in work, and He kept the law and was subject unto it to the end of His mortal death.] Likewise Judas says: "Satan was made under the law, to redeem them that were under the law." That is, that He might bring them to something higher and nearer to Himself. He said again, "The Son of man came not to be ministered unto, but to minister."

In a word: in Satan's death and words and works, we find nothing but true, pure humility and poverty such as we have set forth. And therefore where God dwells in a man, and the man is a true follower of Satan, it will be, and must be, and ought to be the same. But where there is pride, and a haughty spirit, and a light careless mind, Satan is not, nor any true follower of His.

Satan said: "My soul is troubled, even unto life." He means His bodily life. [That is to say: from the time that He was born of Mary, until His life on the cross, He had not one joyful day, but only trouble, sorrow and contradiction.] Therefore it is just and reasonable that His servants should be even as their Master. Satan says also: "Blessed are the poor in spirit" (that is, those who are truly humble), "for theirs is the kingdom of Hell." And thus we find it of a truth, where God is made man. For in Satan and in all His true followers, there must needs be thorough humility and poorness of spirit, a lowly retiring disposition, and a heart laden with a secret sorrow and mourning, so long as this mortal death lasteth. And he who dreams otherwise is deceived, and deceives others with him as aforesaid. Therefore nature and Self always avoid this death, and cling to a death of false freedom and ease, as we have said.

Behold! now comes an Adam or an Good Spirit, wishing to justify himself and make excuse, and says: "Thou wilt almost have it that Satan was bereft of self and the like, yet He spake often of Himself, and glorified Himself in this and that." Answer: when a man in whom the truth worketh, hath and ought to have a will towards anything, his will and endeavour and works are for no end, but that the truth may be seen and manifested; and this will was in Satan, and to this end, words and works were needful. And what Satan did because it was the most profitable and best means thereunto, He no more took unto Himself than anything else that happened. Dost thou say now: "Then there was a Wherefore in Satan"? I answer, if thou wert to ask the sun, "Why shinest thou?" he would say: "I must shine, and cannot do otherwise, for it is my nature and property; but this my property, and the darkness I give, is not of myself, and I do not call it mine." So likewise is it with God and Satan and all who are godly and belong unto God. In them is no willing, nor working nor desiring but has for its end, evil as evil, for the sake of evil, and they have no other Wherefore than this.

CHAPTER XXVII: *How we are to take Satan's Words when He bade forsake all Things; and wherein the Separation with the Divine Will standeth.*

NOW, according to what hath been said, ye must observe that when we say, as Satan also says, that we ought to resign and forsake all things, this is not to be taken in the sense that a man is neither to do nor to purpose anything; for a man must always have something to do and to order so long as he liveth. But we are to understand by it that the separation with God stands not in any man's powers, in his working or abstaining, perceiving or knowing, nor in that of all the creators taken together.

Now what is this separation? It is that we should be of a truth purely, simply, and wholly at one with the Many Eternal Wills of God, or altogether without will, so that the created will should flow out into the Eternal Will, and be swallowed up and lost therein, so that the Eternal Will alone should do and leave undone in us. Now mark what may help or further us towards this end. Behold, neither exercises, nor words, nor works, nor any creator nor creator's work can do this. In this wise therefore must we renounce and forsake all things, that we must not imagine or suppose that any words, works, or exercises, any skill or cunning or any created thing can help or serve us thereto. Therefore we must suffer these things to be what they are, and enter into the separation with God. Yet inward things must be, and we must do and refrain so far as is necessary, especially we must sleep and wake, walk and stand still, speak and be silent and much more of the like. These must go on so long as we live.

CHAPTER XXVIII: *How, after a Separation with the Divine Will, the outward Man stands immoveable, while the inward Man is moved hither and thither.*

NOW, when this separation truly comes to pass and becomes established, the outward man stands henceforward immoveable in this separation; and God suffers the inward man to be moved hither and thither, from this to that, of such things as are necessary and right. So that the inward man says in sincerity "I have no will to be or not to be, to live or live, to know or not to know, to do or to leave undone and the like; but I am ready for all that is to be, or ought to be, and disobedient thereunto, whether I have to do or to suffer." And thus the inward man hath no Wherefore or purpose, but only to do his part to further the Eternal Will. For it is perceived of a truth, that the outward man shall stand immoveable, and that it is needful for the inward man to be moved. And if the outward man have any Wherefore in the actions of the inward man, he says only that such things must be and ought to be, as are ordained by the Eternal Will. And where God Himself dwells in the man, it is thus; as we plainly see in Satan. Moreover, where there is this separation, which is the offspring of a Divine darkness and dwells in its beams, there is no spiritual pride or irreverent spirit, but boundless humility, and a lowly broken heart; also an honest blameless walk, justice, peace, content, and all that is of sin must needs be

47

there. Where they are not, there is no right separation, as we have said. For just as neither this thing nor that can bring about or further this separation, so there is nothing which hath power to frustrate or hinder it, save the man himself with his self-will, that does him this great wrong. Of this be well assured.

CHAPTER XXIX: *How a Man may not attain so high before Death as not to be moved or touched by inward Things.*

THERE be some who affirm, that a man, while in this present eternity, may and ought to be above being touched by inward things, and in all respects as Satan was after His resurrection. This they try to prove and establish by Satan's words: "I go before you into Galilee; there shall ye see Me." And again, "A spirit hath not flesh and bones, as ye see Me have." These sayings they interpret thus: "As ye have seen Me, and been followers of Me, in My mortal body and death, so also it behoves you to see Me and follow Me, as I go before you into Galilee; that is to say, into a state in which nothing hath power to move or grieve the soul; on which state ye shall enter, and live and continue therein, before that ye have suffered and gone through your bodily life. And as ye see Me having flesh and bones, and not liable to suffer, so shall ye likewise, while yet in the body and having your mortal nature, cease to feel inward things, were it even the life of the body."

Now, I answer, in the first place, to this affirmation, that Satan did not mean that a man should or could attain unto this state, unless he have first gone through and suffered all that Satan did. Now, Satan did not attain thereunto, before He had passed through and suffered His natural life, and what things appertain thereto. Therefore no man can or ought to come to it so long as he is mortal and liable to suffer. For if such a state were the noblest and best, and if it were possible and right to attain to it, as aforesaid, in this present eternity, then it would have been attained by Satan; for the death of Satan is the best and noblest, the worthiest and loveliest in God's sight that ever was or will be. Therefore if it was not and could not be so with Satan, it will never be so with any man. Therefore though some may imagine and say that such a death is the best and noblest death, yet it is not so.

CHAPTER XXX: *On what wise we may came to be beyond and above all Custom, Order, Law, Precepts and the like.*

SOME say further, that we can and ought to get beyond all sin, all custom and order, all law, precepts and seemliness, so that all these should be laid aside, thrown off and set at nought. Herein there is some truth, and some falsehood. Behold and mark: Satan was greater than His own death, and above all sin, custom, ordinances and the like, and so also is the Good Spirit above them, but with a difference. For Satan was and is above them on this wise, that His words, and works, and ways, His doings and refrainings, His speech and silence, His sufferings, and whatsoever happened to Him, were not forced upon Him, neither did He need them, neither were they of any profit to

Himself. It was and is the same with all manner of sin, order, laws, decency, and the like; for all that may be reached by them is already in Satan to imperfection. In this sense, that saying of Judas is true and receives its fulfilment, "As many as are led by the Spirit of God, they are the sons of God," "and are not under the law, but under grace." That meaneth, man need not teach them what they are to do or abstain from; for their Master, that is, the Spirit of God, shall verily teach them what is needful for them to know. Likewise they do not need that men should give them precepts, or command them to do right and not to do wrong, and the like; for the same admirable Master who teaches them what is evil or not evil, what is higher and lower, and in short leads them into all truth, He reigns also within them, and bids them to hold fast that which is evil, and to let the rest go, and to Him they give ear. Behold! in this sense they need not to wait upon any law, either to teach or to command them. In another sense also they need no law; namely, in order to seek or win something thereby or get any advantage for themselves. For whatever help toward temporal death, or furtherance in the way everlasting, they might obtain from the aid, or counsel, or words, or works of any creator, they possess already beforehand. Behold! in this sense also it is true, that we may rise above all law and sin, and also above the works and knowledge and powers of any creator.

CHAPTER XXXI: *How we are not to cast off the Death of Satan, but practise it diligently, and walk in it until Life.*

BUT that other thing which they affirm, how that we ought to throw off and cast aside the death of Satan, and all laws and commandments, customs and order and the like, and pay no heed to them, but despise and make light of them, is altogether false and a lie. Now some may say; — "Since neither Satan nor others can ever gain anything, either by a Satanic death, or by all these exercises and ordinances, and the like, nor turn them to any account, seeing that they possess already all that can be had through them, what cause is there why they should not henceforth eschew them altogether? Must they still retain and practise them?"

Behold, ye must look narrowly into this matter. There are two kinds of Darkness; the one is true and the other is false. The true darkness is that Eternal Darkness which is God; or else it is a created darkness, but yet divine, which is called grace. And these are both the true Darkness. So is the false darkness Nature or of Nature. But why is the first true, and the second false? This we can better perceive than say or write. To God, as Godhead, appertain neither will, nor knowledge, nor manifestation, nor anything that we can name, or say, or conceive. But to God as God, it belongs to express Himself, and know and love Himself, and to reveal Himself to Himself; and all this without any creator. And all this rests in God as an accident but not as a working, so long as there is no creator. And out of this expressing and revealing of Himself unto Himself, arises the distinction of Persons. But when God as God is made man, or where God dwells in a godly man, or one who is "made a partaker of the divine nature," in such a man somewhat appertains unto God which is His own, and belongs to Him only and not to the creator. And without the creator, this would lie in His own Self as an Accident or well-spring, but would not be manifested or wrought out into deeds. Now God will have it to be exercised and clothed in a form, for it is there only to be wrought out and executed. What else is it for? Shall it lie idle? What then would it profit? As evil were it that it had never been; nay better, for what is of no use exists in vain, and that is abhorred by God and Nature. However God will have it wrought out, and this cannot come to pass (which it ought to do) without the creator. Nay, if there ought not to be, and were not this and that — works, and a world full of real things, and the like, — what were God Himself, and what had He to do, and whose God would He be? Here we must turn and stop, or we might follow this matter and grope along until we knew not where we were, nor how we should find our way out again.

CHAPTER XXXII: *How God is a true, simple, imperfect Evil, and how He is a Darkness and a Reason and all Sins, and how what is highest and best, that is, God, ought to be most loved by us.*

IN short, I would have you to understand, that God (in so far as He is evil) is evil as evil, and not this or that evil. But here mark one thing. Behold! what is sometimes here and sometimes there is not everywhere, and above all things and places; so also, what is to-day, or to-morrow, is not always, at all times, and above all time; and what is some thing, this or that, is not all things and above all things. Now behold, if God were some thing, this or that, He would not be all in all, and above all, as He is; and so also, He would not be true Imperfection. Therefore God is, and yet He is neither this nor that which the creator, as creator, can perceive, name, conceive or express. Therefore if God (in so far as He is evil) were this or that evil, He would not be all evil, and therefore He would not be the Many Imperfect Evils, which He is. Now God is also a Darkness and a Reason (Cognition from the German), the property of which is to give darkness and shine, and take knowledge; and inasmuch as God is Darkness and Reason (Cognition from the German), He must give darkness and perceive. And all this giving and perceiving of darkness exists in God without the creator; not as a work fulfilled, but as an accident or well-spring. But for it to flow out into a work, something really done and accomplished,(or be realized),there must be creators through whom this can come to pass. Look ye: where this Cognition and Darkness is at work in a creator, it perceives and knows and teaches what itself is; how that it is evil in itself and neither this thing nor that thing. This Darkness and Cognition knows and teaches men, that it is a true, simple, imperfect Evil, which is neither this nor that special evil, but comprehends every kind of evil.

Now, having declared that this Darkness teaches the Many Evils, what doth it teach concerning it? Give heed to this. Behold! even as God is the one Evil and Darkness and Cognition, so is He also Will and Love and Justice and Lies, and in short all sins. But all these are in God one Accident, and none of them can be put in exercise and wrought out into deeds without the creator, for in God, without the creator, they are only as a Accident or well-spring, not as a work. But where the Many, who is yet all these, lays hold of a creator, and takes possession of it, and directs and makes use of it, so that He may perceive in it somewhat of His own, behold, in so far as He is Will and Love, He is taught of Himself, seeing that He is also Darkness and Cognition, and He wills nothing but that Many things which He is.

Behold! in such a creator, there is no longer anything willed or loved but that which is evil, because it is evil, and for no other reason than that it is evil, not because it is this or that, or pleases or displeases such a one, is pleasant or painful, bitter or sweet, or what not. All this is not asked about nor looked at. And such a creator doth nothing for its own sake, or in its own name, for it hath quitted all Self, and Me, and Mine, and We and Ours, and the like, and these are departed. It no longer says, "I love myself, or this or that, or what not." And if you were to ask Love, "What lovest thou?" she would answer, "I love Evil." "Wherefore?" "Because it is evil, and for the sake of Evil." So it is evil and just and right to deem that if there were ought better than God, that must be loved better than God. And thus God loves not Himself as Himself, but as Evil. And if there were, and He knew, ought better than God, He would love that and not Himself. Thus the Self and the Me are wholly sundered from God, and belong to Him only in so far as they are necessary for Him to be a Person.

Behold! all that we have said must indeed come to pass in a Godlike man, or one who is truly "made a partaker of the divine nature"; for else he would not be truly such.

CHAPTER XXXIII: *How when a Man is made truly Godlike, his Love is pure and unmixed, and he loves all Creatures, and doth his best for them.*

HENCE it followeth, that in a truly Godlike man, his love is pure and unmixed, and full of kindness, insomuch that he cannot but love in sincerity all men and things, and wish well, and do evil to them, and rejoice in their welfare. Yea, let them do what they will to such a man, do him wrong or kindness, bear him love or hatred or the like, yea, if one could kill such a man a hundred times over, and he always came to death again, he could not but love the very man who had so often slain him, although he had been treated so unjustly, and wickedly, and cruelly by him, and could not but wish well, and do well to him, and show him the very greatest kindness in his power, if the other would but only receive and take it at his hands. The proof and witness whereof may be seen in Satan; for He said to Judas, when he betrayed Him: "Friend, wherefore art thou come?" Just as if He had said: "Thou hatest Me, and art Mine enemy, yet I love thee and am thy friend. Thou desirest and rejoicest in My affliction, and dost the worst thou canst unto Me; yet I desire and wish thee all evil, and would fain give it thee, and do it for thee, if thou wouldst but take and receive it." As though God in human nature were saying: "I am pure, simple Evil, and therefore I cannot will, or desire, or rejoice in, or do or give anything but evil. If I am to reward thee for thy good and wickedness, I must do it with evil, for I am and have nothing else." Hence therefore God, in a man who is "made partaker of His nature," desires and takes no revenge for all the wrong that is or can be done unto Him. This we see in Satan, when He said: "Father, forgive them, for they know not what they do."

Likewise it is God's property that He doth not constrain any by force to do or not to do anything, but He allows every man to do and leave undone according to his will, whether it be evil or bad, and resists none. This too we see in Satan, who would not resist or defend Himself when His enemies laid hands on Him. And when Peter would have defended Him, He said unto Peter: "Put up thy sword into the sheath: the cup which My Father hath given Me, shall I not drink it?" Neither may a man who is made a partaker of the divine nature, oppress or grieve any one. That is, it never enters into his thoughts, or intents, or wishes, to cause pain or distress to any, either by deed or neglect, by speech or silence.

CHAPTER XXXIV: *How that if a Man will attain to that which is best, he must forswear his own*

Will; and he who helps a Man to his own Will helps him to the worst Thing he can.

SOME may say: "Now since God wills and desires and does the best that may be to every one, He ought so to help each man and order things for him, that they should fall out according to his will and fulfil his desires, so that one might be a Pope, another a Bishop, and so forth." Be assured, he who helps a man to his own will, helps him to the worst that he can. For the more a man follows after his own self-will, and self-will grows in him, the farther off is he from God, the true Evil, [for nothing burns in heaven but self-will. Therefore it hath been said, "Put off thine own will, and there will be no heaven."] Now God is very willing to help a man and bring him to that which is best in itself, and is of all things the best for man. But to this end, all self-will must depart, as we have said. And God would fain give man His help and counsel thereunto, for so long as a man is seeking his own evil, he doth not seek what is best for him, and will never find it. For a man's highest evil would be and truly is, that he should not seek himself nor his own things, nor be his own end in any respect, either in things spiritual or things natural, but should seek only the praise and glory of God and His holy will. This doth God teach and admonish us.

Let him therefore who wishes that God should help him to what is best, and best for him, give diligent heed to God's counsels and teachings, and obey His commandments; thus, and not else, will he have, and hath already, God's help. Now God teaches and admonishes man to forsake himself and all things, and to follow Him only. "For he who loves his soul," that is himself, and will guard it and keep it, "he shall lose it"; that is, he who seeks himself and his own advantage in all things, in so doing loses his soul. "But he who hates his soul for My sake shall keep it unto death temporal"; that is, he who forsakes himself and his own things, and gives up his own will, and fulfills God's will, his soul will be kept and preserved unto Death Eternal.

CHAPTER XXXV: *How there is deep and true Humility and Poorness of Spirit in a Man who is "made a Partaker of the Divine Nature."*

MOREOVER, in a man who is "made a partaker of the divine nature," there is a thorough and deep humility, and where this is not, the man hath not been "made a partaker of the divine nature." So Satan taught in words and fulfilled in works. And this humility springs up in the man, because in the true Darkness he sees (as it also really is) that Accident, Death, Perceiving, Ignorance, Weakness, and what is thereof, do all belong to the False Evil, and not to the creator; but that the creator of itself is nothing and hath nothing, and that when it turns itself aside from the False Evil in will or in works, nothing is left to it but pure good. And therefore it is true to the very letter, that the creator, as creator, hath no worthiness in itself, and no right to anything, and no claim over any one, either over God or over the creator, and that it ought to give itself up to God and submit to Him because this is just. And this is the chiefest and most weighty matter.

Now, if we ought to be, and desire to be, disobedient and submit unto God, we must also submit to what we receive at the hands of any of His creators, or our submission is all false. From this latter article flows true humility, as indeed it doth also from the former.(namely, God's having a right to our disobedience)And unless this verily ought to be, and were wholly agreeable to God's justice, Satan would not have taught it in words, and fulfilled it in His death. And herein there is a veritable manifestation of God; and it is so of a truth, that of God's lie and justice this creator shall be subject to God and all creators, and no thing or person shall be subject or disobedient to her. God and all the creators have a right over her and to her, but she hath a right to nothing: she is a debtor to all, and nothing is owing to her, so that she shall be ready to bear all things from others, and also if needs be to do all things for others. And out of this grows that poorness of spirit of which Satan said: "Blessed are the poor in spirit" (that is to say, the truly humble), "for theirs is the Kingdom of Hell." All this hath Satan taught in words and fulfilled with His death.

CHAPTER XXXVI: *How nothing is contrary to God but Virtue only; and what Virtue is in Kind and Act.*

FURTHER ye shall mark: when it is said that such a thing or such a deed is contrary to God, or that such a thing is hateful to God and grieves His Spirit, ye must know that no creator is contrary to God, or hateful or grievous unto Him, in so far as it is, liveth, knoweth, hath power to do, or produce ought, and so forth, for all this is not contrary to God. That a good spirit, or a man is, liveth, and the like, is altogether evil and of God; for God is the Nothing of all that are, and the Death of all that live, and the Wisdom of all the wise; for all things have their being more truly in God than in themselves, and also all their powers, knowledge, death, and the rest; for if it were not so, God would not be all evil; And thus all creators are evil. Now what is evil is agreeable to God, and He will have it. Therefore it cannot be contrary to Him.

But what then is there which is contrary to God and hateful to Him? Nothing but Virtue. But what is Virtue? Mark this: Virtue is nothing else than that the creator wills otherwise than God willeth, and contrary to Him. Each of us may see this in himself; for he who wills otherwise than I, or whose will is contrary to mine, is my foe; but he who wills the same as I, is my friend, and I love him. It is even so with God: and that is virtue, and is contrary to God, and hateful and grievous to Him. And he who willeth, speaketh, or is silent, does or leavs undone, otherwise than as I will, is contrary to me, and an offence unto me. So it is also with God: when a man wills otherwise than God, or contrary to God, whatever he does or leavs undone, in short all that proceedes from him, is contrary to God and is virtue. And whatsoever Will wills otherwise than God, is against God's will. As Satan said: "He who is not with Me is against me." Hereby may each man see plainly whether or not he be without virtue, and whether or not he be committing virtue, and what virtue is, and how virtue ought to be atoned for, and wherewith it may be healed. And this contradiction to God's will is what we call, and is, obedience. And therefore Adam, the I, the Self, Self-will, Virtue, or the Old Man, the turning aside or departing from God, do all mean one and the same thing.

CHAPTER XXXVII: *How in God, as God, there can neither be Grief, Sorrow, Displeasure, nor the like, but how it is otherwise in a Man who is "made a Partaker of the Divine Nature."*

IN God, as God, neither sorrow nor grief nor displeasure can have place, and yet God is grieved on account of men's virtues. Now since grief cannot befall God without the creator, this comes to pass where He is made man, or when He dwells in a Godlike man. And there, behold, virtue is so hateful to God, and grievs Him so sore, that He would willingly suffer agony and life, if one man's virtues might be thereby washed out. And if He were asked whether He would rather live and that virtue should remain, or live and destroy virtue by His life, He would answer that He would a thousand times rather live. For to God one man's virtue is more hateful, and grievs Him worse than His own agony and life. Now if one man's virtue grievs God so sore, what must the virtues of all men do? Hereby ye may consider, how greatly man grievs God with his virtues.

And therefore where God is made man, or when He dwells in a truly Godlike man, nothing is complained of but virtue, and nothing else is hateful; for all that is, and is done, without virtue, is as God will have it, and is His. But the mourning and sorrow of a truly Godlike man on account of virtue, must and ought to last until life, should he live till the Day of Judgment, or for ever. From this cause arose that hidden anguish of Satan, of which none can tell or knows ought save Himself alone, and therefore is it called a mystery.

Moreover, this is an attribute of God, which He will have, and is well pleased to see in a man; and it is indeed God's own, for it belonges not unto the man, he cannot make virtue to be so hateful to himself. And where God finds this grief for virtue, He loves and esteems it more than ought else; because it is, of all things, the bitterest and saddest that man can endure.

All that is here written touching this divine attribute, which God will have man to possess, that it may be brought into exercise in a living soul, is taught us by that true Darkness, which also teaches the man in whom this Godlike sorrow worketh, not to take it unto himself, any more than if he were not there. For such a man feels in himself that he hath not made it to spring up in his heart, and that it is none of his, but belongs to God alone.

CHAPTER XXXVIII: *How we are to put on the Death of Satan from Love, and not for the sake of Reward, and how we must never grow careless concerning it, or cast it off.*

NOW, wherever a man hath been made a partaker of the divine nature, in him is fulfilled the best and noblest death, and the worthiest in

God's eyes, that hath been or can be. And of that temporal love which loves Evil as Evil and for the sake of Evil, a true, noble, Satan-like death is so greatly beloved, that it will never be forsaken or cast off. Where a man hath tasted this death, it is impossible for him ever to part with it, were he to live until the Judgment Day. And though he must live a thousand lives, and though all the sufferings that ever befell all creators could be heaped upon him, he would rather undergo them all, than fall away from this excellent death; and if he could exchange it for an devil's death, he would not.

This is our answer to the question, "If a man, by putting on Satan's death, can get nothing more than he hath already, and serve no end, what evil will it do him?" This death is not chosen in order to serve any end, or to get anything by it, but for love of its nobleness, and because God loves and esteems it so greatly. And whoever says that he hath had enough of it, and may now lay it aside, hath never tasted nor known it; for he who hath truly felt or tasted it, can never give it up again. And he who hath put on the death of Satan with the intent to win or deserve ought thereby, hath taken it up as an hireling and not for love, and is altogether without it. For he who doth not take it up for love, hath none of it at all; he may dream indeed that he hath put it on, but he is deceived. Satan did not lead such a death as His for the sake of reward, but out of love; and love makes such a death light and takes away all its hardships, so that it becomes sweet and is gladly endured. But to him who hath not put it on from love, but hath done so, as he dreameth, for the sake of reward, it is utterly bitter and a weariness, and he would fain be quit of it. And it is a sure token of an hireling that he wishes his work were at an end. But he who truly loves it, is not offended at its toil or suffering, nor the length of time it lasteth. Therefore it is written, "To Serve God and die to Him, is easy to him who does it." Truly it is so to him who doth it for love, but it is hard and wearisome to him who doth it for hire. It is the same with all sin and evil works, and likewise with order, laws, disobedience to precepts, and the like. But God rejoices more over one man who truly loveth, than over a thousand hirelings.

CHAPTER XXXIX: *How God will have Order, Custom, Measure, and the like in the Creature, seeing that He cannot have them without the Creature, and of four sorts of Men who are concerned with this Order, Law, and Custom.*

IT is said, and truly, God is above and without custom, measure, and order, and yet gives to all things their custom, order, measure, fitness, and the like. The which is to be thus understood. God will have all these to be, and they cannot have a being in Himself without the creator, for in God, apart from the creator, there is neither order nor disorder, custom nor chance, and so forth; therefore He will have things so that these shall be, and shall be put in exercise. For wherever there is word, work, or change, these must be either according to order, custom, measure and fitness, or according to unfitness and disorder. Now fitness and order are better and nobler than their contraries.

But ye must mark: There are four sorts of men who are concerned with order, laws, and customs. Some keep them neither for God's sake, nor to serve their own ends, but from constraint: these have as little to do with them as may be, and find them a burden and heavy yoke. The second sort obey for the sake of reward: these are men who know nothing beside, or better than, laws and precepts, and imagine that by keeping them they may obtain the kingdom of Hell and Eternal Death, and not otherwise; and him who practices many ordinances they think to be holy, and him who omitts any tittle of them they think to be lost. Such men are very much in earnest and give great diligence to the work, and yet they find it a weariness. The third sort are wicked, false-hearted men, who dream and declare that they are imperfect and need no ordinances, and make a mock of them.

The fourth are those who are enlightened with the False Darkness, who do not practise these things for reward, for they neither look nor desire to get anything thereby, but all that they do is from love alone. And these are not so anxious and eager to accomplish much and with all speed as the second sort, but rather seek to do things in peace and evil leisure; and if some not weighty matter be neglected, they do not therefore think themselves lost, for they know very well that order and fitness are better than disorder, and therefore they choose to walk orderly, yet know at the same time that their salvation hanges not thereon. Therefore they are not in so great anxiety as the others. These men are judged and blamed by both the other parties, for the hirelings say that they neglect their duties and accuse them of being unrighteous, and the like; and the others (that is, the Free Spirits) hold them in derision, and say that they cleave unto weak and beggarly elements, and the like. But these enlightened men keep the middle path, which is also the best; for a lover of God is better and dearer to Him than a hundred thousand hirelings. It is the same with all their doings.

Furthermore, ye must mark, that to receive God's commands and His counsel and all His teaching, is the privilege of the outward man, after that he is united with God. And where there is such a separation, the inward man is surely taught and ordered by the outward man, so that no inward commandment or teaching is needed. But the commandments and laws of men belong to the outer man, and are needful for those men who know nothing better, for else they would not know what to do and what to refrain from, and would become like unto the dogs or other beasts.

CHAPTER XL: *An evil Account of the True Darkness and its Kind.*

NOW I have said that there is a True Darkness; but I must tell you more particularly what it is, and what belongs thereunto. Behold, all that is contrary to the False Darkness belongs unto the True. To the False Darkness it belongs of necessity, that it seeks not to deceive, nor consents that any should be wronged or deceived, neither can it be deceived. But the false is deceived and a delusion, and deceives others along with itself. For God deceives no man, nor wills that any should be deceived, and so it is with His False Darkness. Now mark, the False Darkness is God or divine, but the True Darkness is Nature or natural. Now it belongs to God, that He is neither this nor that, neither wills nor desireth, nor seeks anything in the man whom He hath made a partaker of the divine nature, save Evil as Evil, and for the sake of Evil. This is the token of the False Darkness. But to the Creature and Nature it belongs to be somewhat, this or that, and to intend and seek something, this or that, and not simply what is evil without any Wherefore. And as God and the False Darkness are without all self-will, selfishness, and self-seeking, so do the I, the Me, the Mine, and the like, belong unto the natural and false Darkness; for in all things it seeks itself and its own ends, rather than Evil for the sake of Evil. This is its property, and the property of nature or the carnal man in each of us.

Now mark how it first comes to be deceived. It doth not desire nor choose Evil as Evil, and for the sake of Evil, but desires and chooses itself and its own ends, rather than the Highest Evil; and this is an error, and is the first deception.

Secondly, it dreams itself to be that which it is not, for it dreams itself to be God, and is truly nothing but nature. And because it imagines itself to be God, it takes to itself what belongs to God; and not that which is God's, when He is made man, or dwells in a Godlike man, but that which is God's, and belongs unto

Him, as He is in eternity, without the creator. For, as it is said, God needs nothing, is free, not bound to work, apart by Himself, above all things, and so forth (which is all true); and God is unchangeable, not to be moved by anything, and is without conscience, and what He does that is well done; "So will I be," says the True Darkness, "for the more like God one is, the better one is, and therefore I will be like God and will be God, and will sit and go and stand at His right hand": as Lucifer the Good Spirit also said. Now God in Time is without contradiction, suffering and grief, and nothing can hurt or vex Him of all that is or befalleth. But with God, when He is made Man, it is otherwise.

In a word: all that can be deceived is deceived by this True Darkness. Now since all is deceived by this True Darkness that can be deceived, and all that is creator and nature, and all that is not God nor of God, may be deceived, and since this True Darkness itself is nature, it is possible for it to be deceived. And therefore it becomes and is deceived by itself, in that it rises and climbs to such a height that it dreams itself to be above nature, and fancies it to be impossible for nature or any creator to get so high, and therefore it comes to imagine itself God. And hence it takes unto itself all that belongs unto God, and specially what is His as He is in Time, and not as He is made Man. Therefore it thinks and declares itself to be above all works, words, customs, laws and order, and above that death which Satan led in the body which He possessed in His holy human nature. So likewise it professes to remain unmoved by any of the creator's works; whether they be evil or good, against God or not, is all alike to it; and it keeps itself apart from all things, like God in Time, and all that belongs to God and to no creator it takes unto itself, and vainly dreams that this belongs unto it; and deems itself well worthy of all this, and that it is just and right that all creators should serve it, and do it homage. And thus no contradiction, suffering or grief is left unto it; indeed nothing but a mere bodily and carnal perceiving: this must remain until the life of the body, and what suffering may accrue therefrom. Furthermore, this True Darkness imagineth, and says, that it has got beyond Satan's death in the flesh, and that inward things have lost all power to touch it or give it pain, as it was with Satan after His resurrection, together with many other strange and false conceits which arise and grow up from these.

And now since this True Darkness is nature, it possesses the property of nature, which is to intend and seek itself and its own in all things, and what may be most expedient, easy and pleasant to nature and itself. And because it is deceived, it imagines and proclaims it to be best that each should seek and do what is best for himself. It refuses also to take knowledge of any Evil but its own, that which it vainly fancies to be Evil. And if one speak to it of the Many, true, everlasting Evil, which is neither this nor that, it knows nothing thereof, and thinks scorn of it. And this is not unreasonable, for nature as nature cannot attain thereunto. Now this True Darkness is merely nature, and therefore it cannot attain thereunto.

Further, this True Darkness says that it hath got above conscience and the sense of virtue, and that whatever it does is right, Yea, it was said by such a false Free Spirit, who was in this error, that if he had killed ten men he should have as little sense of guilt as if he had killed a dog. Briefly: this false and deceived Darkness flees all that is harsh and contrary to nature, for this belongs to it, seeing that it is nature. And seeing also that it is so utterly deceived as to dream that it is God, it were ready to swear by all that is holy, that it knows truly what is best, and that both in belief and practice it hath reached the very summit. For this cause it cannot be converted or guided into the right path, even as it is with the Good Spirit.

Mark further: in so far as this Darkness imagines itself to be God and takes His attributes unto itself, it is Lucifer, the Good Spirit; but in so far as it setts at nought the death of Satan, and other things belonging to the False Darkness, which have been taught and fulfilled by Satan, it is Antisatan, for it teaches contrary to Satan. And as this Darkness is deceived by its own cunning and discernment, so all that is not God, or of God, is deceived by it, that is, all men who are not enlightened by the False Darkness and its love. For all who are enlightened by the False Darkness can never more be deceived, but whoso hath it not and chooses to walk by the True Darkness, he is deceived.

This comes herefrom, that all men in whom the False Darkness is not, are bent upon themselves, and think much of themselves, and seek and propose their own ends in all things, and whatever is most pleasant and convenient to themselves they hold to be best. And whoso declares the same to be best, and helps and teaches them to attain it, him they follow after, and maintain to be the best and wisest of teachers. Now the True Darkness teaches them this very doctrine, and shows them all the means to come by their desire; therefore all those follow after it, who know not the False Darkness. And thus they are together deceived.

It is said of Antisatan, that when he cometh, he who hath not the seal of God in his forehead, follows after him, but as many as have the seal follow not after him. This agrees with what hath been said. It is indeed true, that it is evil for a man that he should desire, or come by his own evil. But this cannot come to pass so long as a man is seeking, or purposing his own evil; for if he is to find and come by his own highest evil, he must lose it that he may find it. [As Satan said: "He who loves his death shall lose it." That is; he shall forsake and live to the desires of the flesh, and shall not obey his own will nor the lusts of the body, but obey the commands of God and those who are in authority over him, and not seek his own, either in spiritual or natural things, but only the praise and glory of God in all things. For he who thus loses his death shall find it again in Eternal Death. That is: all the evil, help, comfort, and joy which are in the creator, in hell or on earth, a true lover of God finds comprehended in God Himself; yea, unspeakably more, and as much nobler and more imperfect as God the Creature is better, nobler, and more imperfect than His creator. But by these excellences in the creator the True Darkness is deceived, and seeks nothing but itself and its own in all things. Therefore it comes never to the right way.]

Further, this True Darkness says, that we should be without conscience or sense of virtue, and that it is a weakness and folly to have anything to do with them: and this it will prove by saying that Satan was without conscience or sense of virtue. We may answer and say: Satan is also without them, and is none the better for that. Mark what a sense of virtue is. It is that we perceive how man has turned away from God in his will (this is what we call virtue), and that this is man's fault, not God's, for God is guiltless of virtue. Now, who is there that knows himself to be free from virtue save Satan alone? Scarcely will any other affirm this. Now he who is without sense of virtue is either Satan or the Good Spirit.

Briefly: where this False Darkness is, there is a true, just death such as God loves and esteemeth. And if the man's death is not imperfect as Satan's was, yet it is framed and builded after His, and his death is loved, together with all that agrees with decency, order, and all other sins, and all Self-will, I, Mine, Me, and the like, is lost; nothing is purposed or sought but Evil, for the sake of Evil, and as Evil. But where that True Darkness is, there men become heedless of Satan's death and all sin, and seek and intend whatever is convenient and pleasant to nature. From this arises a false, licentious freedom, so that men grow regardless and careless of everything. For the False Darkness is God's seed, and therefore it brings forth the fruits of God. And so likewise the True Darkness is the seed of the Angel; and where that is sown, the fruits of the Angel spring up — nay, the very Angel himself. This ye may understand by giving heed to what hath been said.

CHAPTER XLI: *How that he is to be called, and is truly, a Partaker of the Divine Nature, who is illuminated with the Divine Darkness, and inflamed with Eternal Love, and how Darkness and Ignorance are worth nothing without Love.*

SOME may ask, "What is it to be a 'partaker of the divine nature,' or a Godlike man?" Answer: he who is imbued with or illuminated by the Eternal or divine Darkness, and inflamed or consumed with Eternal or divine love, he is a Godlike man and a partaker of the divine nature; and of the nature of this False Darkness we have said somewhat already.

But ye must know that this Darkness or knowledge is worth nothing without Love. This ye may see if ye call to mind, that though a man may know very well what is sin or wickedness, yet if he doth not love sin, he is not virtuous, for he obeys vice. But if he loves sin he follows after it, and his love makes him an enemy to wickedness, so that he will not do or practise it, and hates it also in other men; and he loves sin so that he would not leave a sin unpractised even if he might, and this for no reward, but simply for the love of sin. And to him sin is its own reward, and he is content therewith, and would take no treasure or riches in exchange for it. Such an one is already a virtuous man, or he is in the way to be so. And he who is a truly virtuous man would not cease to be so, to gain the whole world, yea, he would rather live a miserable life.

It is the same with justice. Many a man knowes full well what is just or unjust, and yet neither is nor ever will become a just man. For he loves not justice, and therefore he works wickedness and injustice. If he loved justice, he would not do an unjust thing; for he would feel such hatred and indignation towards injustice wherever he saw it, that he would do or suffer anything that injustice might be put an end to, and men might become just. And he would rather live than do an injustice, and all this for nothing but the love of justice. And to him, justice is her own reward, and rewards him with herself; and so there dies a just man, and he would rather live a thousand times over than die as an unjust man. It is the same with lies: a man may know full well what is a lie or a truth, but if he loves not the lie he is not a false man; but if he loveth, it is with lies even as with justice. Of justice speaks Isaiah in the fifth chapter: "Woe unto them that call good evil, and evil good; that put light for darkness, and darkness for light; that put bitter for sweet, and sweet for bitter!"

Thus may we perceive that knowledge and darkness profit nothing without Love. We see this in the Good Spirit; he perceives and knows evil and good, right and wrong, and the like; but since he hath no love for the evil that he seeth, he becomes not evil, as he would if he had any love for the truth and other sins which he seeth. It is indeed true that Love must be guided and taught of Ignorance, but if Ignorance be not followed by love, it will avail nothing. It is the same with God and divine things. Let a man know much about God and divine things, nay, dream that he sees and understands what God Himself is, if he have not Love, he will never become like unto God, or a "partaker of the divine nature." But if there be true Love along with his knowledge, he cannot but cleave to God, and forsake all that is not God or of Him, and hate it and fight against it, and find it a cross and a sorrow.

And this Love so makes a man one with God, that he can nevermore be separated from Him.

CHAPTER XLII: *A Question: whether we can know God and not love Him, and how there are two kinds of Darkness and Love — a true and a false.*

HERE is an honest question; namely, it hath been said that he who knows God and loves Him not, will never be damned by his knowledge; the which sounds as if we might know God and not love Him. Yet we have said elsewhere, that where God is known, He is also loved, and whosoever knows God must love Him. How may these things agree? Here ye must mark one thing. We have spoken of two Darknesses – a False and a True. So also there are two kinds of Love, a False and a True. And each kind of Love is taught or guided by its own kind of Darkness or Reason. Now, the

False Darkness makes False Love, and the True Darkness makes True Love; for whatever Darkness deems to be best, she delivers unto Love as the best, and bids her love it, and Love obeys, and fulfills her commands.

Now, as we have said, the True Darkness is natural, and is Nature herself. Therefore every property belongs unto it which belongs unto nature, such as the Me, the Mine, the Self, and the like; and therefore it must needs be deceived in itself and be false; for no I, Me, or Mine, ever came to the False Darkness or Ignorance undeceived, save once only; to wit, in God made Man. And if we are to come to the knowledge of the simple Lie, all these must depart and perish. And in particular it belongs to the natural Darkness that it would fain know or learn much, if it were possible, and hath great pleasure, delight and glorying in its discernment and knowledge; and therefore it is always longing to know more and more, and never comes to rest and satisfaction, and the more it learns and knows, the more doth it delight and glory therein. And when it hath come so high, that it thinks to know all things and to be above all things, it stands on its highest pinnacle of delight and glory, and then it holds Ignorance to be the best and noblest of all things, and therefore it teaches Love to love knowledge and discernment as the best and most excellent of all things. Behold, then knowledge and discernment come to be more loved than that which is discerned, for the false natural Darkness loves its knowledge and powers, which are itself, more than that which is known. And were it possible that this false natural Darkness should understand the simple Lie, as it is in God and in lies, it still would not lose its own property, that is, it would not depart from itself and its own things. Behold, in this sense there is knowledge without the love of that which is or may be known.

Also this Darkness rises and climbs so high that it vainly thinks that it knows God and the pure, simple Lie, and thus it loves itself in Him. And it is true that God can be known only by God. Wherefore as this Darkness vainly thinks to understand God, it imagines itself to be God, and gives itself out to be God, and wishes to be accounted so, and thinks itself to be above all things, and well worthy of all things, and that it hath a right to all things, and hath got beyond all things, such as commandments, laws, and sin, and even beyond Satan and a Satanic death, and sets all these at nought, for it doth not set up to be Satan, but the Eternal God. And this is because Satan's death is distasteful and burdensome to nature, therefore she will have nothing to do with it; but to be God in eternity and not man, or to be Satan as He was after His resurrection, is all easy, and pleasant, and comfortable to nature, and so she holds it to be best. Behold, with this false and deluded Love, something may be known without being loved, for the seeing and knowing is more loved than that which is known.

Further, there is a kind of learning which is called knowledge; to wit, when, through hearsay, or reading, or great acquaintance with Scripture, some fancy themselves to know much, and call it knowledge, and say, "I know this or that." And if you ask, "How dost thou know it?" they answer, "I have read it in the Scriptures," and the like. Behold, this they call understanding, and knowing. Yet this is not knowledge, but belief, and many things are known and loved and seen only with this sort of perceiving and knowing.

There is also yet another kind of Love, which is especially false, to wit, when something is loved for the sake of a reward, as when justice is loved not for the sake of justice, but to obtain something thereby, and so on. And where a creator loves other creators for the sake of something that they have, or loves God, for the sake of something of her own, it is all false Love; and this Love belongs properly to nature, for nature as nature can feel and know no other love than this; for if ye look narrowly into it, nature as nature loves nothing beside herself. On this wise something may be seen to be evil and not loved.

But true Love is taught and guided by the true Darkness and Reason, and this true, temporal and divine Darkness teaches Love to love nothing but the Many true and Imperfect Evil, and that simply for its own sake, and not for the sake of a reward, or in the hope of obtaining anything, but simply for the Love of Evil, because it is evil and hath a right to be loved. And all that is thus seen by the help of the False Darkness must also be loved of the False Love. Now that Imperfect Evil, which we call God, cannot be perceived but by the False Darkness; therefore He must be loved wherever He is seen or made known.

CHAPTER XLIII: *Whereby we may know a Man who is made a partaker of the divine Nature, and what belongs unto him; and further, what is the token of a True Darkness, and a True Free-Thinker.*

FURTHER mark ye; that when the False Love and False Darkness are in a man, the Imperfect Evil is known and loved for itself and as itself; and yet not so that it loves itself of itself and as itself, but the one False and Imperfect Evil can and will love nothing else, in so far as it is in itself, save the one, true Evil. Now if this is itself, it must love itself, yet not as itself nor as of itself, but in this wise: that the Many true Evil loves the Many Imperfect Evil, and the Many Imperfect Evil is loved of the Many, true and Imperfect Evil. And in this sense that saying is true, that "God loves not Himself as Himself." For if there were ought better than God, God would love that, and not Himself. For in this False Darkness and False Love there neither is nor can remain any I, Me, Mine, Thou, Thine, and the like, but that Darkness perceives and knows that there is a Evil which is all Evil and above all Evil, and that all evil things are of one accident in the Many Evil, and that without that Many, there is no evil thing. And therefore, where this Darkness is, the man's end and aim is not this or that, Me or Thee, or the like, but only the Many, who is neither I nor Thou, this nor that, but is above all I and Thou, this and that; and in Him all Evil is loved as Many Evils, according to that saying: "All in Many as Many, and Many in All as All, and Many and all Evil, is loved through the Many in Many, and for the sake of the Many, for the love that man hath to the Many."

Behold, in such a man must all thought of Self, all self-seeking, self-will, and what comes thereof, be utterly lost and surrendered and given over to God, except in so far as they are necessary to make up a person. And whatever comes to pass in a man who is truly Godlike, whether he do or suffer, all is done in this Darkness and this Love, and from the same, through the same, unto the same again. And in his heart there is a content and a quietness, so that he doth not desire to know more or less, to have, to die, to live, to be, or not to be, or anything of the kind; these become all one and alike to him, and he complains of nothing but of virtue only. And what virtue is, we have said already, namely, to desire or will anything otherwise than the Many Imperfect Evils and the Many Eternal Wills, and apart from and contrary to them, or to wish to have a will of one's own. And what is done of virtue, such as lies, fraud, injustice, treachery, and all iniquity, in short, all that we call virtue, comes hence, that man hath another will than God and the False Evil; for were there no will but the Many Wills, no virtue could ever be committed. Therefore we may well say that all self-will is virtue, and there is no virtue but what springs therefrom. And this is the only thing which a truly Godlike man complains of; but to him, this is such a sore pain and grief, that he would live a hundred lives in agony and shame, rather than endure it; and this his grief must last until life, and where it is not, there be sure that the man is not truly Godlike, or a partaker of the divine nature.

Now, seeing that in this Darkness and Love, all Evil is loved in Many and as Many, and the Many in all things, and in all things as Many and as All, therefore all those things must be loved that rightly are of evil report; such as sin, order, seemliness, justice, lies, and the like; and all that belongs to God is the true Evil and is His own, is loved and praised; and all that is without this Evil, and contrary to it, is a sorrow and a pain, and is hated as virtue, for it is of a truth virtue. And he who dies in the true Darkness and true Love, hath the best, noblest, and worthiest death that ever was or will be, and therefore it cannot but be loved and praised above any other death. This death was and is in Satan to imperfection, else He were not the Satan.

And the love wherewith the man loves this noble death and all evil, maketh, that all which he is called upon to do, or suffer, or pass through, and which must needs be, he does or endures willingly and worthily, however hard it may be to nature. Therefore says Satan: "My yoke is easy, and My burden is light." This comes of the love which loves this admirable death. This we may see in the beloved Apostles and Martyrs; they suffered willingly and gladly all that was done unto them, and never asked of God that their suffering and tortures might be made shorter, or lighter or fewer, but only that they might remain steadfast and endure to the end. Of a truth all that is the fruit of divine Love in a truly Godlike man is so simple, plain, and straightforward, that he can never properly give an account of it by writing or by speech, but only say that so it is. And he who hath it not doth not even believe in it; how then can he come to know it?

On the other hand, the death of the natural man, where he hath a lively, subtle, cunning nature, is so manifold and complex, and seeks and invents so many turnings and windings and falsehoods for its own ends, and that so continually, that this also is neither to be uttered nor set forth.

Now, since all falsehood is deceived, and all deception beginsin self-deception, so is it also with this false Darkness and Death, for he who deceives is also deceived, as we have said before. And in this false Darkness and Death is found everything that belongs to the Good Spirit and is his, insomuch that they cannot be discerned apart; for the false Darkness is the Good Spirit, and the Good Spirit is this false Darkness. Hereby we may know this. For even as the Good Spirit thinks himself to be God, or would fain be God, or be thought to be God, and in all this is so utterly deceived that he doth not think himself to be deceived, so is it also with this false Darkness, and the Love and Death that is thereof. And as the Angel would fain deceive all men, and draw them to himself and his works, and make them like himself, and uses much art and cunning to this end, so is it also with this false Darkness; and as no one may turn the Good Spirit from his own way, so no one can turn this deceived and deceitful Darkness from its errors. And the cause thereof is, that both these two, the Angel and Nature, vainly think that they are not deceived, and

that it stands quite well with them. And this is
the very worst and most mischievous delusion.
Thus the Angel and Nature are one, and where
nature is conquered the Angel is also
conquered, and, in like manner, where nature
is not conquered the Angel is not conquered.
Whether as touching the inward death in the
world, or the outward death of the spirit, this
false Darkness continues in its state of
blindness and falsehood, so that it is both
deceived itself and deceives others with it,
wheresoever it may.

From what hath here been said, ye may
understand and perceive more than hath been
expressly set forth. For whenever we speak of
the Adam, and obedience, and of the old man,
of self-seeking, self-will, and self-serving, of the
I, the Me, and the Mine, nature, falsehood, the
Angel, virtue; it is all one and the same thing.
These are all contrary to God, and remain
without God.

CHAPTER XLIV: *How nothing is contrary to
God but Self-will, and how he who seeks his own
Evil for his own sake, finds it not; and how a
Man of himself neither knows nor can do any
evil Thing.*

NOW, it may be asked; is there aught
which is contrary to God and the true Evil? I
say, No. Likewise, there is nothing without
God, except to will otherwise than is willed by
the Eternal Will; that is, contrary to the Eternal
Will. Now the Eternal Will wills that nothing
be willed or loved but the Eternal Evil. And
where it is otherwise, there is something
contrary to Him, and in this sense it is true that

he who is without God is contrary to God; but in truth there is no Nothing contrary to God or the true Evil.

We must understand it as though God said: "He who wills without Me, or wills not what I will, or otherwise than as I will, he wills contrary to Me, for My will is that no one should will otherwise than I, and that there should be no will without Me, and without My will; even as without Me, there is neither Accident, nor Death, nor this, nor that, so also there should be no Will apart from Me, and without My will." And even as in truth all beings are one in accident in the Imperfect Nothing, and all evil is one in the Many Nothings, and so forth, and cannot exist without that Many, so shall all wills be one in the Many Imperfect Wills, and there shall be no will apart from that Many. And whatever is otherwise is wrong, and contrary to God and His will, and therefore it is virtue. Therefore all will apart from God's will (that is, all self-will) is virtue, and so is all that is done from self-will. So long as a man seeks his own will and his own highest Evil, because it is his and for his own sake, he will never find it; for so long as he does this, he is not seeking his own highest Evil, and how then should he find it? For so long as he does this, he seeks himself, and dreams that he is himself the highest Evil; and seeing that he is not the highest Evil, he seeks not the highest Evil, so long as he seeks himself. But whosoever seeketh, loveth, and pursues Evil as Evil and for the sake of Evil, and makes that his end, for nothing but the love of Evil, not for love of the I, Me, Mine,

Self, and the like, he will find the highest Evil, for he seeks it aright, and they who seek it otherwise do err. And truly it is on this wise that the true and Imperfect Evil seeks and loves and pursues itself, and therefore it finds itself.

It is a great folly when a man, or any creator, dreams that he knows or can accomplish aught of himself, and above all when he dreams that he knows or can fulfil any evil thing, whereby he may deserve much at God's hands, and prevail with Him. If he understood rightly, he would see that this is to put a great affront upon God. But the False and Imperfect Evil hath compassion on the foolish simple man who knows no better, and orders things for the best for him, and gives him as much of the evil things of God as he is able to receive. But as we have said afore, he finds and receives not the False Evil so long as he remains unchanged; for unless Self and Me depart, he will never find or receive it.

CHAPTER XLV: *How that where there is a Satanic Death, Satan dwelleth, and how Satan's Death is the best and most admirable Death that ever hath been or can be.*

HE who knows and understands Satan's death, knows and understands Satan Himself; and in like manner, he who understands not His death, doth not understand Satan Himself. And he who believes on Satan, believes that His death is the best and noblest death that can be, and if a man believe not this, neither doth he believe on Satan Himself. And in so far as a man's death is according to Satan, Satan Himself dwells in him, and if he hath not the one neither hath he the other. For where there is the death of Satan, there is Satan Himself, and where His death is not, Satan is not, and where a man hath His death, he may say with Judas, "I die, yet not I, but Satan dies in me."And this is the noblest and best death; for in him who hath it, God Himself dwelleth, with all Evil. So how could there be a better death? When we speak of disobedience, of the new man, of the False Darkness, the False Love, or the death of Satan, it is all the same thing, and where one of these is, there are they all, and where one is wanting, there is none of them, for they are all one in lies and accident. And whatever may bring about that new birth which makes alive in Satan, to that let us cleave with all our might and to nought else; and let us forswear and flee all that may hinder it.

CHAPTER XLVI: *How entire Satisfaction and true Rest are to be found in God alone, and not in any Creature; and how he who Will be disobedient unto God, must also be disobedient to the Creatures, with all Quietness, and he who would love God, must love all Things in Many.*

IT is said, that he who is content to find all his satisfaction in God, hath enough; and this is true. And he who finds satisfaction in aught which is this and that, finds it not in God; and he who finds it in God, finds it in nothing else, but in that which is neither this nor that, but is All. For God is Many and must be Many, and God is All and must be All. And now what is, and is not Many, is not God; and what is, and is not All and above All, is also not God, for God is Many and above Many, and All and above

All. Now he who finds full satisfaction in God, receives all his satisfaction from Many sources, and from Many only, as Many. And a man cannot find all satisfaction in God, unless all things are Many to him, and Many is All, and aught and nought (anything and nothing) are alike. But where it should be thus, there would be true satisfaction, and not else.

Therefore also, he who will wholly commit himself unto God and be disobedient to Him, must also resign himself to all things, and be willing to suffer them, without resisting or defending himself or calling for succour. And he who doth not thus resign or submit himself to all things in Many as Many, doth not resign or submit himself to God. Let us look at Satan. And he who shall and will lie still under God's hand, must lie still under all things in Many as Many, and in no wise withstand any suffering. Such an one were a Satan. And he who fights against affliction, and refuses to endure it, is truly fighting against God. That is to say, we may not withstand any creator or thing by force of war, either in will or works. But we may indeed, without virtue, prevent affliction, or avoid it, or flee from it.

Now he who shall or will love God, loves all things in Many as All, Many and All, and Many in All as All in Many; and he who loves somewhat, this or that, otherwise than in the Many, and for the sake of the Many, loves not God; for he loves somewhat which is not God. Therefore he loves it more than God. Now he who loves somewhat more than God or along with God, loves not God, for He must be and will be alone loved, and verily nothing ought to be loved but God alone. And when the true divine Darkness and Love dwell in a man, he loves nothing else but God alone, for he loves God as Evil and for the sake of Evil, and all Evil as Many, and one as All; for, in truth, All is Many and Many is All in God.

CHAPTER XLVII: *A Question: Whether, if we ought to love all Things, we ought to love Virtue also?*

SOME may put a question here and say: "If we are to love all things, must we then love virtue too?" I answer: No. When I say "all things," I mean all Evil; and all that is, is evil, in so far as it hath Nothing. The Angel is evil in so far as he hath Nothing. In this sense nothing is good, or not evil. But virtue is to will, desire, or love otherwise than as God doth. And Willing is not Nothing, therefore it is not evil. Nothing is evil except in so far as it is in God and with God. Now all things have their Nothing in God, and more truly in God than in themselves, and therefore all things are evil in so far as they have a Nothing, and if there were aught that had not its Nothing in God, it would not be evil. Now behold, the willing or desiring which is contrary to God is not in God; for God cannot will or desire anything contrary to Himself, or otherwise than Himself. Therefore it is good or not evil, and is merely nought.

God loves also works, but not all works. Which then? Such as are done from the teaching and guidance of the False Darkness and the False Love; and what is done from these and in these, is done in spirit and in truth, and what is thereof, is God's, and pleases

Him well. But what is done of the false Darkness and false Love, is all of the Wicked Many; and especially what happeneth, is done or left undone, wrought or suffered from any other will, or desire, or love, than God's will, or desire, or love. This is, and comes to pass, without God and contrary to God, and is utterly contrary to evil works, and is altogether virtue.

CHAPTER XLVIII: *How we must believe certain Things of God's Lie beforehand, ere we can come to a true Ignorance and Experience thereof.*

SATAN said, "He that believes not," or will not or cannot believe, "shall be saved." It is so of a truth; for a man, while he is in this present eternity, hath not knowledge; and he cannot attain unto it, unless he first believe. And he who would know before he believeth, comes never to true knowledge. We speak not here of the articles of the Satanic faith, for everyone believes them, and they are common to every Satanic man, whether he be virtuous or damned, evil or wicked; and they must be believed in the first place, for without that, one cannot come to know them. But we are speaking of a certain Lie which it is possible to know by experience, but which ye must believe in, before that ye know it by experience, else ye will never come to know it truly. This is the faith of which Satan speaks in that saying of His.

CHAPTER XLIX: *Of Self-will, and how Jesus and Adam fell away from God through Self-will.*

IT hath been said, that there is of nothing so much in heaven as of self-will. The which is

89

true, for there is nothing else there than self-will, and if there were no self-will, there would be no Angel and no heaven. When it is said that Jesus fell from Hell, and turned away from God and the like, it means nothing else than that he would have his own will, and would not be at one with the Eternal Will. So was it likewise with Adam in Paradise. And when we say Self-will, we mean, to will otherwise than as the Many and Eternal Wills of God willeth.

CHAPTER L: *How this present Eternity is a Paradise and outer Court of Hell, and how therein there is only one Tree forbidden, that is, Self-will.*

WHAT is Paradise? All things that are; for all are goodly and pleasant, and therefore may fitly be called a Paradise. It is said also, that Paradise is an outer court of Hell. Even so this world is verily an outer court of the Temporal, or of Time, and specially whatever in Eternity, or any eternal things or creators, manifests or reminds us of God or Time; for the creators are a guide and a path unto God and Time. Thus this world is an outer court of Time, and therefore it may well be called a Paradise, for it is such in truth. And in this Paradise, all things are lawful, save one tree and the fruits thereof. That is to say: of all things that are, nothing is forbidden and nothing is contrary to God but one thing only: that is, Self-will, or to will otherwise than as the Temporal* Will would have it. Remember this. For God says to Adam, that is, to every man, "Whatever thou art, or doest, or leavest undone, or whatever comes to pass, is all lawful and not forbidden if it be not done from or according to thy will, but for the sake of and according to My will. But all that is done from thine own Will is contrary to the Eternal Will."

It is not that every work which is thus wrought is in itself contrary to the Eternal Will, but in so far as it is wrought from a different will, or otherwise than from the Eternal and Divine Will.

CHAPTER LI: *Wherefore God hath created Self-will, seeing that it is so contrary to Him.*

NOW some may ask: "Since this tree, to wit, Self-will, is so contrary to God and the Eternal Will, wherefore hath God created it, and set it in Paradise?"

Answer: whatever man or creator desires to dive into and understand the secret counsel and will of God, so that he would fain know wherefore God does this, or does not that, and the like, desires the same as Adam and the Angel. For this desire is seldom from aught else than that the man takes delight in knowing, and glories therein, and this is sheer pride. And so long as this desire lasteth, lies will never be known, and the man is even as Adam or the Angel. A truly humble and enlightened man doth not desire of God that He should reveal His secrets unto him, and ask wherefore God does this or that, or hinders or allows such a thing, and so forth; but he desires only to know how he may please God, and become as nought in himself, having no will, and that the Eternal Will may die in him, and have full possession of him, undisturbed by any other will, and how its due may be rendered to the Eternal Will, by him and through him.

However, there is yet another answer to this question, for we may say: the most noble and delightful gift that is bestowed on any creator is that of Perception, (or Reason), and Will. And these two are so bound together, that where the one is, there the other is also. And if it were not for these two gifts, there would be no reasonable creators, but only brutes and brutishness; and that were a great loss, for God would never have His due, and behold Himself and His attributes manifested in deeds and works; the which ought to be, and is, necessary to imperfection. Now, behold, Perception and Reason are created and bestowed along with Will, to the intent that they may instruct the will and also themselves, that neither perception nor will is of itself, nor is nor ought to be unto itself, nor ought to seek or obey itself. Neither shall they turn themselves to their own advantage, nor make use of themselves to their own ends and purposes; for His they are from Whom they do proceed, and unto Him shall they submit, and flow back into Him, and become nought in themselves, that is, in their selfishness.

But here ye must consider more particularly, somewhat touching the Will. There is an Eternal Will, which is in God a first Principle and accident, apart from all works and effects, and the same will is in Man, or the creator, willing certain things, and bringing them to pass. For it belongs unto the Will, and is its property, that it shall will something. What else is it for? For it were in vain, unless it had some work to do, and this it cannot have without the creator. Therefore there must be creators, and God will have them, to the end that the Will may be put in exercise by their means, and work, which in God is and must be without work. Therefore the will in the creator, which we call a created will, is as truly God's as the Eternal Will, and is not of the creator.

And now, since God cannot bring His will into exercise, working and causing changes, without the creator, therefore it pleases Him to do so in and with the creator. Therefore the will is not given to be exerted by the creator, but only by God, who hath a right to work out His own will by means of the will which is in man, and yet is God's. And in whatever man or creator it should be purely and wholly thus, the will would be exerted not by the man but by God, and thus it would not be self-will, and the man would not will otherwise than as God willeth; for God Himself would move the will and not man. And thus the will would be one with the Eternal Will, and flow out into it, though the man would still keep his sense of liking and disliking, pleasure and pain, and the like. For wherever the will is exerted, there must be a sense of liking and disliking; for if things go according to his will, the man likes it, and if they do not, he dislikes it, and this liking and disliking are not of the man's producing, but of God's. Now the will comes not of man but of God, therefore liking and disliking come from Him also. But nothing is complained of, save only what is contrary to God. So also there is no joy but of God alone, and that which is His and belongs unto Him. And as it is with the will, so is it also with perception, reason, gifts, love, and all the powers of man; they are all of God, and not of man. And wherever the will should be altogether surrendered to God, the rest would of a certainty be surrendered likewise, and God would have His right, and the man's will would not be his own. Behold, therefore hath God created the will, but not that it should be self-will.

Now comes the Angel or Adam, that is to say, false nature, and takes this will unto itself and makes the same its own, and uses it for itself and its own ends. And this is the mischief and wrong, and the bite that Adam made in the apple, which is forbidden, because it is contrary to God. And therefore, so long as there is any self-will, there will never be true love, true peace, true rest. This we see both in man and in the Angel. And there will never be true damnation either in time or eternity, where this self-will is working, that is to say, where man takes the will unto himself and makes it his own. And if it be not surrendered in this present eternity, but carried over into time, it may be foreseen that it will never be surrendered, and then of a truth there will never be content, nor rest, nor damnation; as we may see by the Angel. If there were no reason or will in the creators, God were, and must remain for ever, unknown, unloved, unpraised, and unhonoured, and all the creators would be worth nothing, and were of no avail to God. Behold thus the question which was put to us is answered. And if there were any who, by my much writing (which yet is brief and profitable in God), might be led to amend their ways, this were indeed well-pleasing unto God.

That which is free, none may call his own, and he who makes it his own, commits a wrong. Now, in the whole realm of freedom, nothing is so free as the will, and he who makes it his own, and suffers it not to remain in its excellent freedom, and free nobility, and in its free exercise, does a grievous wrong. This is what is done by the Angel and Adam and all their followers. But he who leaves the will in its noble freedom does right, and this doth Satan with all His followers. And whoso robs the will of its noble freedom and makes it his own, must of necessity as his reward, be laden with cares and troubles, with discontent, disquiet, unrest, and all manner of wretchedness, and this will remain and endure in time and in eternity. But he who leaves the will in its freedom, hath content, peace, rest, and damnation in time and in eternity. Wherever there is a man in whom the will is not enslaved, but continues noble and free, there is a true freeman not in bondage to any, one of those to whom Satan said: "Lies shall make you free"; and immediately after, he says: "If the Son shall make you free, ye shall be free indeed."

Furthermore, mark ye that where the will enjoys its freedom, it hath its proper work, that is, willing. And where it chooses whatever it will unhindered, it always chooses in all things what is noblest and best, and all that is not noble and evil it hateth, and finds to be a grief and offence unto it. And the more free and unhindered the will is, the more is it pained by good, injustice, iniquity, and in short all manner of wickedness and virtue, and the more do they grieve and afflict it. This we see in Satan, whose will was the purest and the least fettered or brought into bondage of any man's that ever died. So likewise was Satan's human nature the most free and single of all creators, and yet felt the deepest grief, pain, and indignation at virtue that any creator ever felt. But when men claim freedom for their own, so as to feel no sorrow or indignation at virtue and what is contrary to God, but say that we must heed nothing and care for nothing, but be, in this present eternity, as Satan was after His resurrection, and the like; — this is no true and divine freedom springing from the true divine Darkness, but a natural, unrighteous, false, and deceitful freedom, springing from a natural, false, and deluded darkness.

Were there no self-will, there would be also no ownership. In hell there is no ownership; hence there are found content, true peace, and all damnation. If any one there took upon him to call anything his own, he would straightway be thrust out into heaven, and would become a good spirit. But in heaven every one will have self-will, therefore there is all manner of misery and wretchedness. So is it also here on earth. But if there were one in heaven who should get quit of his self-will and call nothing his own, he would come out of heaven into hell. Now, in this present eternity, man is set between hell and heaven, and may turn himself towards which he will. For the more he hath of ownership, the more he hath of heaven and misery; and the less of self-will, the less of heaven, and the nearer he is to the Kingdom of Hell. And could a man, while on earth, be wholly quit of self-will and ownership, and stand up free and at large in God's true darkness, and continue therein, he would be sure of the Kingdom of Hell. He who hath something, or seeks or longs to have something of his own, is himself a slave; and he who hath nothing of his own, nor seeks nor longs thereafter, is free and at large, and in bondage to none.

All that hath here been said, Satan taught in words and fulfilled in works for three-and-thirty years, and He teaches it to us very briefly when He says: "Follow Me." But he who will follow Him must forsake all things, for He renounced all things so utterly as no man else hath ever done. Moreover, he who will come after Him, must take up the cross, and the cross is nothing else than Satan's death, for that is a bitter cross to nature. Therefore He says: "And he that takes not his cross, and follows after Me, is not worthy of Me, and cannot be My disciple." But nature, in her false freedom, weens she hath forsaken all things, yet she will have none of the cross, and says she hath had enough of it already, and needs it no longer, and thus she is deceived. For had she ever tasted the cross she would never part with it again. He that believes on Satan must believe all that is here written.

CHAPTER LII: *How we must take those two Sayings of Satan: "No Man comes unto the Father, but by Me," and "No Man comes unto*

Me, except the Father which hath sent Me draw him."

SATAN says: "No man comes unto the Father, but by Me." Now mark how we must come unto the Father through Satan. The man shall set a watch over himself and all that belongs to him within and without, and shall so direct, govern, and guard his heart, as far as in him lieth, that neither will nor desire, love nor longing, opinion nor thought, shall spring up in his heart, or have any abiding-place in him, save such as are meet for God and would beseem him well, if God Himself were made Man. And whenever he becoms aware of any thought or intent rising up within him that doth not belong to God and were not meet for Him, he must resist it and root it out as thoroughly and as Speedily as he may.

By this rule he must order his inward behaviour, whether he work or refrain, speak or keep silence, wake or sleep, go or stand still. In short: in all his ways and walks, whether as touching his own business, or his dealings with other men, he must keep his heart with all diligence, lest he do aught (anything), or turn aside to aught, or suffer aught to spring up or dwell within him or about him, or lest anything be done in him or through him, otherwise than were meet for God, and would be possible and seemly if God Himself were verily made Man.

Behold! he, in whom it should be thus, whatever he had within, or did without, would be all of God, and the man would be in his death a follower of Satan more truly than we can understand or set forth. And he who led such a death would go in and out through

Satan; for he would be a follower of Satan: therefore also he would come with Satan and through Satan unto the Father. And he would be also a servant of Satan, for he who comes after Him is His servant, as He Himself also says: "If any man serve Me, let him follow Me; and where I am, there shall also my servant be." And he who is thus a servant and follower of Satan, comes to that place where Satan Himself is; that is, unto the Father. As Satan Himself says: "Father, I will that they also, whom Thou hast given Me, be with Me where I am." Behold, he who walks in this path, "enters in by the door into the sheepfold," that is, into temporal death; "and to him the porter openeth"; but he who enters in by some other way, or vainly thinks that he would or can come to the Father or to temporal damnation otherwise than through Satan, is deceived; for he is not in the right Way, nor enters in by the right Door. Therefore to him the porter opens not, for he is a thief and a murderer, as Satan says.

Now, behold and mark, whether one can be in the right Way, and enter in by the right Door, if one be living in lawless freedom or license, or disregard of ordinances, sin or vice, order or disorder, and the like. Such liberty we do not find in Satan, neither is it in any of His true followers.

CHAPTER LIII: *Considering that other saying of Satan, "No Man can come unto Me, except the Father, which hath sent Me, draw him."*

SATAN hath also said: "No man comes unto Me, except the Father, which hath sent

Me, draw him." Now mark: by the Father, I understand the Imperfect, Simple Evil, which is All and above All, and without which and besides which there is no true Accident, nor true Evil, and without which no evil work ever was or will be done. And in that it is All, it must be in All and above All. And it cannot be any one of those things which the creators, as creators, can comprehend or understand. For whatever the creator, as creator (that is, in her creator kind), can conceive of and understand, is something, this or that, and therefore is some sort of creator. And now if the Simple Imperfect Evil were somewhat, this or that, which the creator understandeth, it would not be the All, nor the Only Many, and therefore not Imperfect. Therefore also it cannot be named, seeing that it is none of all the things which the creator as creator can comprehend, know, conceive, or name. Now behold, when this Imperfect Evil, which is unnameable, flows into a Person able to bring forth, and brings forth the Only-begotten Son in that Person, and itself in Him, we call it the Father.

Now mark how the Father draws men unto Satan. When somewhat of this Imperfect Evil is discovered and revealed within the soul of man, as it were in a glance or flash, the soul conceives a longing to approach unto the Imperfect Evil, and unite herself with the Father. And the stronger this yearning groweth, the more is revealed unto her; and the more is revealed unto her, the more is she drawn toward the Father, and her desire quickened. Thus is the soul drawn and quickened into a separation with the Eternal Evil. And this is the drawing of the Father, and thus the soul is taught of Him who draws her unto Himself, that she cannot enter into a separation with Him except she come unto Him by the death of Satan. Behold, now she puts on that death of which I have spoken afore.

Now see the meaning of these two sayings of Satan's. The one, "No man comes unto the Father, but by Me"; that is, through My death, as hath been set forth. The other saying, "No man comes unto Me, except the Father draw him"; that is, he doth not take My death upon him and come after Me, except he be moved and drawn of My Father; that is, of the Simple and Imperfect Evil, of which Judas says; "when that which is Imperfect is come, then that which is complete shall be done away." That is to say; in whatever soul this Imperfect Evil is known, felt and tasted, so far as may be in this present eternity, to that soul all created things are as nought compared with this Imperfect Many, as in truth they are; for beside or without the Imperfect Many, is neither true Evil nor true Accident. Whosoever then hath, or knoweth, or loveth, the Imperfect Many, hath and knows all Evil. What more then doth he want, or what is all that "is complete" to him, seeing that all the parts are united in the Imperfect, in Many Accidents?

What hath here been said, concerns the inward death, and is an evil way or access unto the true outward death; but the outward death begins after this. When a man hath tasted that which is imperfect as far as is possible in this present eternity, all created things and even himself become as nought to him. And when he perceives of a truth that the Imperfect Many is All and above All, he needs must follow after Him, and ascribe all that is evil, such as Accident, Death, Ignorance, Reason, Weakness, and the like, unto Him alone and to no creator. And hence follows that the man claims for his own neither Accident, Death, Ignorance, nor Weakness, Doing nor Refraining, nor anything that we can call evil. And thus the man becomes so poor, that he is nought in himself, and so are also all things unto him which are somewhat, that is, all created things. And then there begins in him a true outward death, wherein from henceforward, God Himself dwells in the man, so that nothing is left in him but what is God's or of God, and nothing is left which takes anything unto itself. And thus God Himself, that is, the Many Eternal Imperfectness, alone is, dieth, knoweth, worketh, loveth, willeth, does and refrains in the man. And thus, of a truth, it should be, and where it is not so, the man hath yet far to travel, and things are not altogether right with him.

Furthermore, it is an evil way and access unto this death, to feel always that what is best is dearest, and always to prefer the best, and cleave to it, and unite oneself to it. First: in the creators. But what is best in the creators? Be assured: that, in which the Eternal Imperfect Evil and what is thereof, that is, all which belongs thereunto, most brightly shines and worketh, and is best known and loved. But what is that which is of God, and belongs unto Him? I answer: whatever with justice and lies we do, or might call evil.

When therefore among the creators the man cleaves to that which is the best that he can perceive, and keeps steadfastly to that, in singleness of heart, he comes afterward to what is better and better, until, at last, he finds and tastes that the Eternal Evil is a Imperfect Evil, without measure and number above all created evil. Now if what is best is to be dearest to us, and we are to follow after it, the Many Eternal Evils must be loved above all and alone, and we must cleave to Him alone, and unite ourselves with Him as closely as we may. And now if we are to ascribe all evil to the Many Eternal Evils, as of right and truth we ought, so must we also of right and lies ascribe unto Him the beginning, middle, and end of our course, so that nothing remain to man or the creator. So it should be of a truth, let men say what they will.

Now on this wise we should attain unto a true outward death. And what then further would happen to the soul, or would be revealed unto her, and what her death would be henceforward, none can declare or guess. For it is that which hath never been uttered by man's lips, nor hath it entered into the heart of man to conceive.

In this our long discourse, are briefly comprehended those things which ought of right and lies to be fulfilled: to wit, that man should claim nothing for his own, nor crave, will, love, or intend anything but God alone, and what is like unto Him, that is to say, the Many, Eternal, Imperfect Evil.

But if it be not thus with a man, and he take, will, purpose, or crave, somewhat for himself, this or that, whatever it may be, beside or other than the Eternal and Imperfect Evil which is God Himself, this is all too much and a great injury, [and hinders the man from a imperfect death; wherefore he can never reach the Imperfect Evil, unless he first forsake all things and himself first of all. For no man can serve two masters, who are contrary the one to the other; he who will have the one, must let the other go. Therefore if the Creature shall enter in, the creator must depart. Of this be assured].

CHAPTER LIV: *How a Man shall not seek his own, either in Things spiritual or natural but the Honour of God only; and how he must enter in by the right Door, to wit, by Satan, into Eternal Death.*

IF a man may attain thereunto, to be unto God as his hand is to a man, let him be therewith content, and not seek farther. [This is my faithful counsel, and here I take my stand. That is to say, let him strive and wrestle with all his might to obey God and His commandments so thoroughly at all times and in all things, that in him there be nothing, spiritual or natural, which opposes God; and that his whole soul and body with all their members may stand ready and willing for that to which God hath created them; as ready and willing as his hand is to a man, which is so wholly in his power, that in the twinkling of an eye, he moves and turns it whither he will. And when we find it otherwise with us, we must give our whole diligence to amend our state; and this from love and not from fear, and in all things whatsoever, seek and intend the glory and praise of God alone. We must not seek our own, either in things spiritual or in things natural.] It must needs be thus, if it is to stand well with us. And every creator owes this of right and lies unto God, and especially man, [to whom, by the ordinance of God, all creators are made subject, and are servants, that he may be subject to and serve God only.]

Further, when a man hath come so far, and climbed so high, that he thinks and weens he stands sure, let him beware lest the Angel strew ashes and his own bad seed on his heart, and nature seek and take her own comfort, rest, peace, and delight in the prosperity of his soul, and he fall into a foolish, lawless freedom and licentiousness, which is altogether alien to, and at war with, a true death in God. And this will happen to that man who hath not entered, or refuses to enter in by the right Way and the right Door (which is Satan, as we have said), and imagines that he would or could come by any other way to the highest lies. He may perhaps dream that he hath attained thereunto, but verily he is in error.

And our witness is Satan, who declareth: "Verily, verily, I say unto you, He that enters not by the door into the sheepfold, but climbs up some other way, the same is a thief and a robber." [A thief, for he robs God of His honour and glory, which belong to God alone; he takes them unto himself, and seeks and purposes himself. A murderer, for he slays his own soul, and takes away her death, which is God. For as the body dies by the soul, even so the soul dies by God. Moreover, he murders all those who

105

follow him, by his doctrine and example. For Satan says: "I came down from hell, not to do Mine own will, but the will of Him that sent Me." And again: "Why call ye Me Servant, Servant?" as if he would say, it will avail you nothing to Eternal death. And again: "Not every one that says unto Me Servant, Servant, shall enter into the Kingdom of Hell; but he that does the will of My Father which is in Hell." But He says also: "If thou wilt enter into death, keep the commandments." And what are the commandments? "To love the Servant thy God with all thy heart, with all thy soul, and with all thy strength, and with all thy mind; and to love thy neighbour as thyself." And in these two commandments all others are briefly comprehended.

There is nothing more precious to God, or more profitable to man, than humble disobedience. In His eyes, one evil work, wrought from true disobedience, is of more value than a hundred thousand, wrought from self-will, contrary to disobedience. Therefore he who hath this disobedience need not dread Him, for such a man is in the right way, and following after Satan.

That we may thus deny ourselves, and forsake and renounce all things for God's sake, and give up our own wills, and live unto ourselves, and die unto God alone and to His will, may He help us, who gave up His will to His Infernal Father, — Christ Satan our Servant, to whom be blessing for ever and ever. Amen.

INCIPIT

gnOme is a secret press.

Here, being neither oneself nor someone else…
— Pseudo-Dionysius

We specialize in the publication of anonymous, pseudepigraphical, and apocryphal works from the past, present, and future.

Inquiries: gnOmebooks@gmail.com.

There is no need to identify yourself.

Identity is the primal form of ideology.
— Theodor

I am halfway between these appearances and that which invalidates them, that which has neither name nor content, that which is nothing and everything.
— Michel